Keyboard Success

Teacher's Guide

Second Edition

Sam Miller
Mary Smith
Ann Fidanque
Gail Sullivan

International Society for Technology in Education
EUGENE, OREGON

Keyboard Success Teacher's Guide, Second Edition

Sam Miller

Mary Smith

Ann Fidanque

Gail Sullivan

Director of Publishing
Jean Marie Hall

Project Coordinator
Diannah Anavir

Acquisitions Editor
Anita McAnear

Copy Editors
Ron Renchler, The Electronic Page
Maggie Wheeler

Technical Editors
Corinne Tan, Tracy Cozzens

Cover & Book Design
Sue Roberts

Hand Model
Kye Thomas Ruddell, age 10

Copyright © 2000 International Society for Technology in Education

World rights reserved. No part of this book may be reproduced or transmitted in any form or by any means—electronic, mechanical, photocopying, recording, or otherwise—without prior written permission from the publisher. For permission, ISTE members contact Permissions Editor, ISTE, 480 Charnelton Street, Eugene, OR 97401-2626; fax: 1.541.434.8948; e-mail: permissions@iste.org. Nonmembers contact Copyright Clearance Center, 222 Rosewood Drive, Danvers, MA 01923; fax: 1.978.750.4744.

An exception to the above statement is made for K–12 classroom materials or teacher training materials contained in this publication and, if applicable, on the accompanying CD-ROM. A single classroom teacher or teacher educator may reproduce these materials for his or her classroom or students' uses. The reproduction of any materials in this publication or on the accompanying CD-ROM for an entire school or school system, or for other than nonprofit educational purposes, is strictly prohibited.

Trademarks: Rather than put a trademark symbol in every occurrence of a trademarked name, we state that we are using the names only in an editorial fashion and to the benefit of the trademark owner, with no intention of infringement of the trademark.

International Society for Technology in Education (ISTE)
480 Charnelton Street
Eugene, OR 97401-2626
Order Desk: 1.800.336.5191
Order Fax: 1.541.302.3778
Customer Service: orders@iste.org
Books and Courseware: books@iste.org
Permissions: permissions@iste.org
World Wide Web: www.iste.org

Second Edition
ISBN 1-56484-152-9

About ISTE

The International Society for Technology in Education (ISTE) is a nonprofit professional organization with a worldwide membership of leaders in educational technology. We are dedicated to promoting appropriate uses of information technology to support and improve learning, teaching, and administration in PK–12 education and teacher education. As part of that mission, ISTE provides high-quality and timely information, services, and materials, such as this book.

The ISTE Publishing Department works with experienced educators to develop and produce classroom-tested books and courseware. We look for content that emphasizes the use of technology where it can make a difference—making the teacher's job easier; saving time; motivating students; helping students who have unique learning styles, abilities, or backgrounds; and creating learning environments that would be impossible without technology. We believe technology can improve the effectiveness of teaching while making learning exciting and fun.

Every manuscript and product we select for publication is peer reviewed and professionally edited. While we take pride in our publications, we also recognize the difficulties of maintaining quality while keeping on top of the latest technologies and research. Please let us know which products you would find helpful. We value your feedback on this book and other ISTE products. E-mail us at **books@iste.org**.

ISTE is home of the National Educational Technology Standards (NETS) Project, the National Educational Computing Conference (NECC), and the National Center for Preparing Tomorrow's Teachers to Use Technology (NCPT^3). To learn more about NETS or request a print catalog, visit our Web site at **www.iste.org**, which provides:

- Current educational technology standards for PK–12 students, teachers, and administrators
- A bookstore with online ordering and membership discount options
- *Learning & Leading with Technology* magazine and the *Journal of Research on Technology in Education*
- *ISTE Update,* online membership newsletter
- Teacher resources
- Discussion groups
- Professional development services, including national conference information
- Research projects
- Member services

About the Authors

Sam Miller teaches middle school science and mathematics, has an extensive background in technology-based education, and is a research associate in the College of Education at the University of Oregon. He has been employed as a curriculum specialist for Lane Education Service District; instructional designer at Utah State University; head teacher for the technology-based da Vinci public alternative school in Eugene; project coordinator for the Apple Classroom of Tomorrow, sponsored by Apple Computer, Inc.; and director of the Oregon US West/NEA Teacher Network.

Mary Smith was born and raised in Eugene, Oregon. She attended Bethel schools and has taught Grades 2 through 5 for the past 29 years in Bethel. She is now teaching fifth grade at Malabon Elementary School and is getting her administrative certificate.

Ann Fidanque, M.A., is a reading teacher and Title 1 coordinator in Eugene, Oregon. She has taught students in kindergarten through sixth grade since 1973. She has held several education positions, including general education teacher, special education teacher, and Title 1 teacher and coordinator. She has co-authored *Read Well*, a beginning reading curriculum (Sopris West, 1998).

Gail Sullivan was a classroom teacher for 21 years in Eugene School District 4J, Eugene, Oregon. She was a computer curriculum specialist and served as Teacher on Special Assignment for Computers for the district for two years, editing a computer newsletter, presenting workshops, and instructing adults and children.

Contents

Introduction 1
   Program Overview 1
   Instructional Objectives 2
   Instructional Approach 2
   Learning Environment 3
   Presenting Lessons 4
   Establishing the Basics 5
   Monitoring and Evaluating Students 7
   Special Needs Students 9
   Teacher Enthusiasm 9
   Scope and Sequence 9

Lesson 1 • Introduction 11
   Handwriting Rate 11
   Finger Naming 13
   Keyboarding Position 16
   Home Key Location 18

Lesson 2 • a SPACEBAR j RETURN 21
   Finger Naming Review 21
   Keyboarding Position Review 22
   Home Key Review 23
   Key Introduction:
      a SPACEBAR j RETURN 24
   Practice 26

Lesson 3 • s k 27
   Finger Naming Review 27
   Key Review 28
   Key Introduction: s k 28
   Practice 31

Lesson 4 • Review 33
   Finger Naming Review 33
   Key Review 34
   Practice 35

Lesson 5 • d l 27
   Key Review 37
   Key Introduction: d l 38
   Practice 40

Lesson 6 • SEMICOLON f 41
   Key Review 41
   Key Introduction: SEMICOLON f 42
   Practice 44

Lesson 7 • Review & Timed Practice 45
   Key Review 45
   Practice 46
   Keyboarding Rate 47
   Calculating Gross Words A Minute
      (GWAM) 49

Lesson 8 • e h 51
   Key Review 51
   Key Introduction: e h 52
   Practice 54

Lesson 9 • Review 55
   Key Review 55
   Practice 56

Lesson 10 • o r 57
   Key Review 57
   Key Introduction: o r 58
   Practice 60

Lesson 11 • Review 61
   Key Review 61
   Practice 62

Lesson 12 • i t 63
   Key Review 63
   Key Introduction: i t 64
   Practice 66

Lesson 13 • Review 67
   Key Review 67
   Practice 68

Lesson 14 • PERIOD COMMA 69
   Key Review 69
   Key Introduction: PERIOD COMMA 70
   Practice 72

Lesson 15 • LEFT SHIFT QUESTION MARK 73
   Key Review 73
   Key Introduction:
      LEFT SHIFT QUESTION MARK 74
   Practice 77

Lesson 16 • Review & Timed Practice 79
   Key Review 79
   Practice 80
   Keyboarding Rate 81
   Calculating Gross Words A Minute
     (GWAM) 83

Lesson 17 • u c 85
   Key Review 85
   Key Introduction: u c 86
   Practice 88

Lesson 18 • Review 89
   Key Review 89
   Practice 90

Lesson 19 • n w 91
   Key Review 91
   Key Introduction: n w 92
   Practice 94

Lesson 20 • g RIGHT SHIFT EXCLAMATION POINT 95
   Key Review 95
   Key Introduction: g RIGHT SHIFT
      EXCLAMATION POINT 96
   Practice 98

Lesson 21 • Review 101
Key Review 101
Practice 102

Lesson 22 • m b 103
Key Review 103
Key Introduction: m b 104
Practice 106

Lesson 23 • Review & Timed Practice 107
Key Review 107
Practice 108
Keyboarding Rate 109
Calculating Gross Words A Minute (GWAM) 111

Lesson 24 • p x 113
Key Review 113
Key Introduction: p x 114
Practice 116

Lesson 25 • Review 117
Key Review 117
Practice 118

Lesson 26 • y z 119
Key Review 119
Key Introduction: y z 120
Practice 122

Lesson 27 • Review 123
Key Review 123
Practice 124

Lesson 28 • q QUOTATION MARK 125
Key Review 125
Key Introduction:
   q QUOTATION MARK 126
Practice 128

Lesson 29 • v APOSTROPHE 129
Key Review 129
Key Introduction: v APOSTROPHE 130
Practice 132

Lesson 30 • Review & Timed Practice 133
Key Review 133
Practice 134
Keyboarding Rate 135
Calculating Gross Words A Minute (GWAM) 137

Appendix 139
References
Handwriting Rate Worksheet
Record Grid for Handwriting and Keyboarding Rates
Position Chart for Good Keyboarding Habits
Finger Naming Worksheet
Keyboard Template
Calculating Gross Words A Minute (GWAM)
Certificate of Completion

Introduction

Welcome to the second edition of *Keyboard Success*, an easy-to-teach curriculum designed to introduce fundamental keyboarding skills to elementary and middle school students. The program is based on a thorough review of technology curriculum standards, keyboarding research, and observations of students using keyboards in the classroom. It is designed to directly teach all students in regular, short, focused sessions.

The revision to this publication comes at a time when the integration of technology into K–12 education has moved beyond the hypothetical. According to the National Educational Technology Standards for Students developed and published by the International Society for Technology in Education (ISTE), students completing fifth grade should be able to use keyboards and other common input and output devices (including adaptive devices when necessary) efficiently and effectively. It is toward that end that this book is dedicated.

Keyboard Success is an introductory curriculum. It does not teach students how to locate number keys, seldom-used characters, or text formatting for compositions. Instead, the curriculum uses a carefully sequenced approach to help students learn proper keyboarding techniques that will increase their proficiency in daily computer applications and build confidence at the keyboard. The program can be used successfully by teachers, parents, peer tutors, or paraprofessionals.

The *Keyboard Success* curriculum does not depend on keyboarding software. While such software may be effective with individual, motivated students, we have found that students who use it exclusively tend to develop the habit of watching their fingers. This not only undermines the recommended keyboarding position but also inhibits the attainment of keyboarding competence. Consequently, we do not recommend keyboarding software for other than additional practice.

Program Overview

Target Audience. *Keyboard Success* is intended for intermediate elementary and middle school students (Grades 3–8), but it has also been successfully used with older students and students with special needs. Keyboard familiarity is useful for younger students, but trying to teach them a formal curriculum is probably not the best use of their learning time.

Program Components. The *Keyboard Success* curriculum includes the following resources:
- ***Teacher's Guide.*** Carefully scripted instructions for each lesson are provided, eliminating the need for special training in presenting the curriculum.
- ***Keyboard Wall Chart.*** This teaching aid helps introduce students to new keys. Color coding connects keys to the fingers used, offering a quick visual reference for students and the instructor. The wall chart also includes cues for the correct keyboarding position, along with illustrative photos.
- ***Student Flip Book.*** This booklet contains the text students enter for each practice lesson and bonus lessons. Each keyboarding student must have a booklet.

Equipment. This curriculum assumes you have the ability to print or save students' timed practice exercises to obtain information on keyboarding rate and accuracy. To benefit fully, students should have access to a computer with word-processing or text-editing capabilities, a word-processing typewriter, a portable keyboard that can save to a computer, or an electric typewriter. Other typing equipment (or even the keyboarding template provided in the appendix of this book) may be used, but you should be alert to the need to eliminate or make adjustments for obtaining rate and accuracy information for the four timed exercises. More information on equipment is provided in the "Learning Environment" section. A clock or watch with a second hand is also needed for the timed practice.

Lesson Length. The curriculum consists of 30 teacher-directed lessons, each of which can be completed in approximately 25 minutes.

Instructional Objectives

Keyboard Success introduces real words as soon as possible, frequently reviews previously taught skills, and provides additional practice for accelerated students. The main instructional objectives are to teach students how to:
- keyboard from a correct body and hand position
- keystroke properly
- develop reasonable keying speed and accuracy

Instructional Approach

Success in implementing this keyboarding curriculum relies on three elements: systematic practice, modeling, and monitoring.

Have Students Practice Systematically. Keyboarding is similar to learning how to play a musical instrument or sport. It's a psychomotor skill that is gradually acquired through the repetition of carefully selected examples. *Keyboard Success* builds skills progressively through daily teacher-directed lessons.

New keystrokes are introduced based on their relative ease of reach in combination with previously introduced keys. To reduce errors in which the correct finger but incorrect hand is used (such as "e" for "i"), keys controlled by the same finger but opposite hand are introduced in different lessons.

Introduction

The lesson examples are carefully distributed so students move as soon as possible from isolated letters, to letter combinations, to meaningful words, phrases, and sentences.

Use Modeling Techniques. An important part of each *Keyboard Success* lesson is your demonstration of correct keyboarding techniques. Illustrations and computer graphics are helpful adjuncts to keyboarding but no substitute for live modeling. While modeling, you can help students understand the goals for each lesson and point out potential areas of difficulty and how to overcome them.

Monitor Your Students. Teaching keyboarding requires your active participation. You should circulate among the students during the lesson, observing their techniques and providing encouragement and additional demonstrations as needed.

Learning Environment

To use this program most successfully, you should give careful consideration to both the physical and instructional environments. In working with the physical environment, it is important to consider the following factors.

Keyboards. Under the best conditions, each student in a classroom would have a computer with a display screen that can be tilted so the student's line of vision is at an angle approaching 90 degrees. If you have different kinds of equipment in the classroom (i.e., different brands of computers, LCD keyboards, typewriters), group similar equipment together to facilitate specific instruction for different groups of learners.

Furniture. Students should have their chairs placed at a height that permits them to sit comfortably with both feet flat on the floor. If necessary, provide a footrest (a box or book) for pupils whose feet do not reach the floor. The keyboard desk or table should be adjusted so that students can easily curve their fingers in the proper position over the HOME keys.

Room Arrangement. The classroom furniture should be arranged so students can easily see you during demonstrations. Aisles should be clear so that you can move easily from student to student. If you plan to use the *Keyboard Wall Chart* for demonstration, it should be visible to each student in the classroom.

Lighting. Make sure computer systems are located in an area in which lighting does not cause glare on the monitors.

Presenting Lessons

It's not necessary to memorize the lesson directions in *Keyboard Success*, but you should review them prior to each lesson. After you've presented several lessons, you'll notice that the lesson procedures remain consistent, and you'll quickly become familiar with the format.

Since the program is intended for a wide range of students, the length of each lesson will vary depending on students' ages and developmental levels. A lesson can usually be presented in 25 minutes or less. If you do not have time to complete a lesson on a given day, simply review and finish the lesson the next day.

Lesson Summary. The lesson directions begin with a summary of keys to be introduced and materials needed to present the lesson. Most of the lessons use the *Keyboard Wall Chart* and *Student Flip Book*. In addition, some lessons require the use of a clock or watch with a second hand for timed practice.

Lesson Format. Lessons have been formatted visually for ease of execution.

Lesson Summary.

Numbering makes it easy to keep your place.

Italic text describes what you do.

Words and letters you read aloud or dictate appear in plain text.

Line length suggests the duration of spoken text.

Keyboard actions and punctuation appear as small capital letters.

Expected student responses appear in brackets following teacher questions.

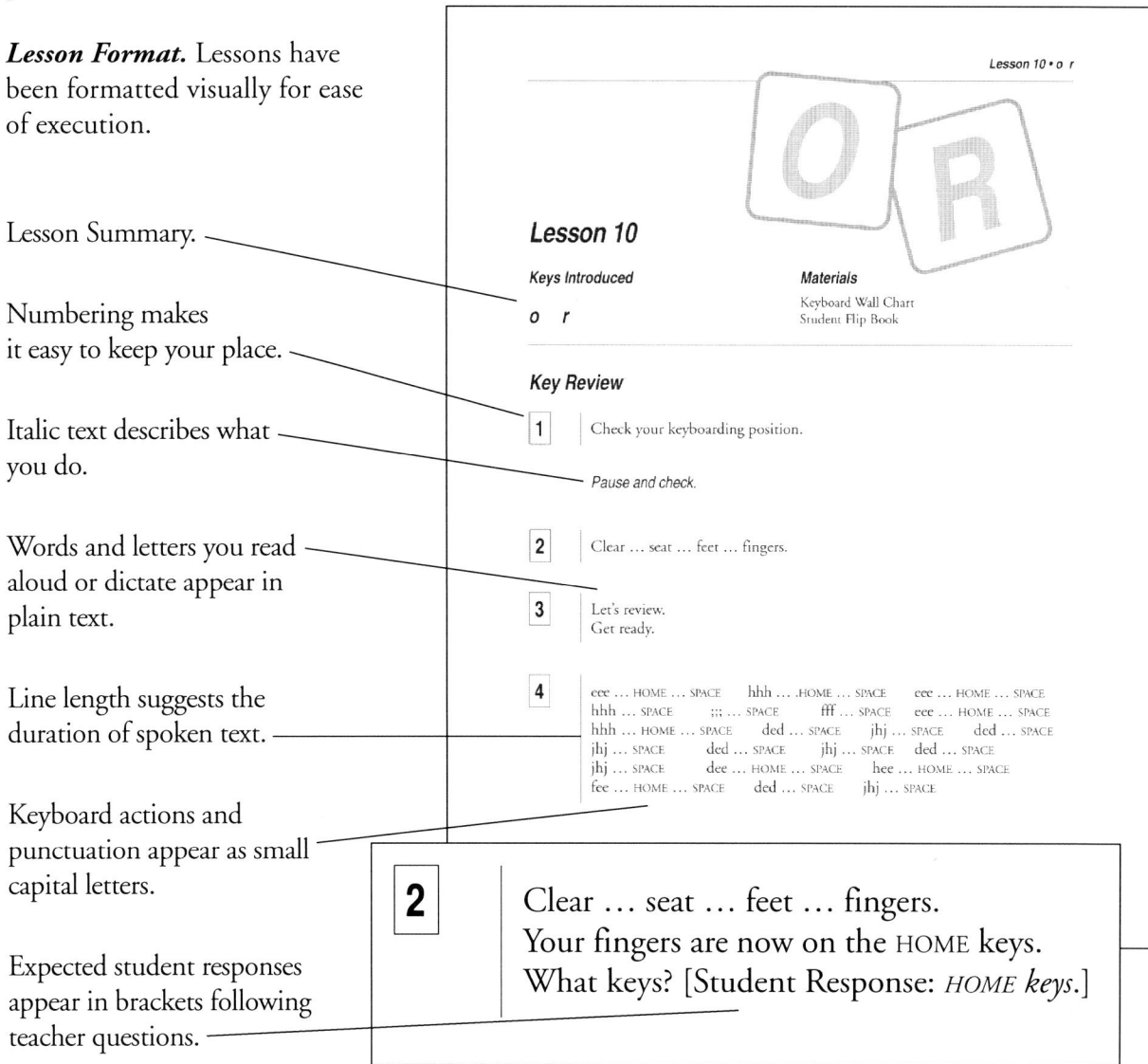

Introduction

Lesson Directions and Content. The lessons are divided into various exercises that you present and guide students through. Lesson directions are carefully worded to present information concisely. Present the lessons verbatim, using a steady pace.

Establishing the Basics

Lesson 1 introduces keyboarding basics—finger naming, correct keyboarding position, and the location of the HOME keys. An exercise to establish each student's handwriting rate is also included in this lesson.

Correct Keyboarding Position. It is important for students to maintain a relaxed and consistent keyboarding position. The Position Chart for Good Keyboarding Habits is included as an appendix to this book and in Lesson 1 of the *Student Flip Book*. The *Keyboard Wall Chart* provides word cues—Clear, Seat, Feet, and Fingers—that you and your students can use for quick reference during instruction.

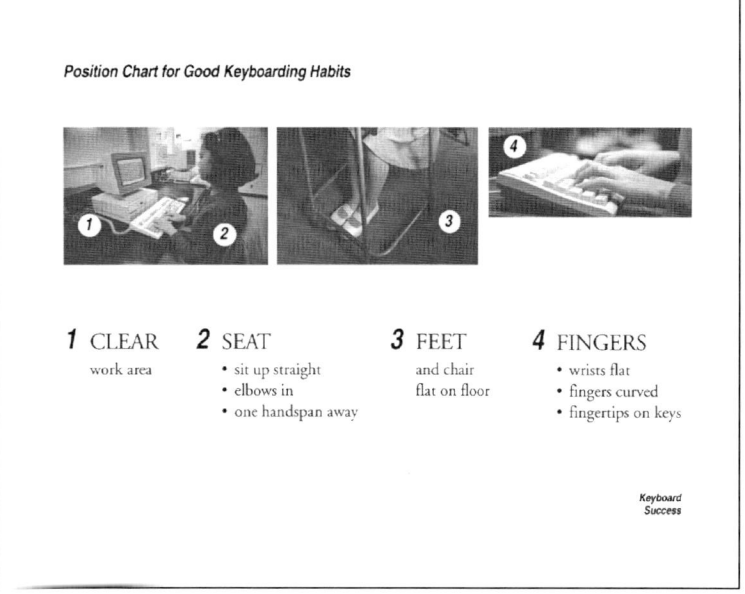

You should ensure that
- Work areas are clear. This eliminates obstacles and distractions.
- Students are sitting up straight in their seats with a slight forward lean. They should be positioned one handspan (palm down with fingers spread as widely as possible) away from the keyboard with the tip of the little finger pointing toward the "j" key. Instruct students to hang their arms at their sides, bend their elbows, and bring their forearms up to the keyboard.
- Students' feet and chairs are flat on the floor. Chairs should be at a proper height for each student and positioned in front of the computers so students can comfortably reach the keys. Smaller students may need footrests.
- Elbows are tucked in, wrists are flat, and fingers are curved over the HOME keys. The back of students' hands should follow the slant of the keyboard. When using the *Student Flip Book*, encourage students to keep their eyes on the copy in their books or on their monitors.

Keyboarding Techniques. Throughout the lessons, you will cue and monitor your students' keyboarding techniques. New techniques are introduced along with new keys. For example, with the introduction of non-HOME keys, students are instructed to anchor and return fingers quickly to the HOME keys. Thereafter, you will monitor students to ensure they are anchoring and returning their fingers to the HOME keys as they keyboard.

In addition to body position, you should demonstrate and monitor the following keyboarding techniques:

- Curved fingers
- Flat wrists
- Backs of hands following the slant of the keyboard
- Still hands
- Light, quick, snappy keystrokes
- Correct reach
- Unused fingers anchored to the HOME keys
- Fingers returned quickly to the HOME keys
- Steady rhythm
- SPACEBAR and RETURN keys pressed quickly
- Eyes on copy or monitor
- Correct fingers used for SHIFT keys

Key Introduction. Thirty-six keys are introduced in 17 lessons throughout the program. Key introductions are the basis for introducing correct finger paths for keystrokes. The *Keyboard Wall Chart* makes it easy to identify key locations and demonstrate correct finger placement and finger paths. (Note that the *Keyboard Wall Chart* labels only the keys that are introduced in this curriculum.) Place the chart in a location visible to all students. For small groups, you may choose to demonstrate the correct keypath on an actual keyboard. Demonstrations are designed to be brief so that students can immediately practice a new keystroke.

Key Review and Practice. With the exception of Lesson 1, all the lessons in *Keyboard Success* include review and practice.

- **Review.** Lessons 2 through 30 include teacher-guided review of previously introduced information and keys. Finger naming is reviewed in Lessons 2 through 4. Lessons 3 through 30 include key reviews. Eight lessons are dedicated entirely to review and practice. All lessons incorporate cues for the correct keyboarding position that has been demonstrated during early lessons.

- **Practice.** Lessons 2 through 30 provide practice exercises. Each of these chapters includes the following types of practice:

Teacher-Dictated Practice. During teacher-dictated practice you read and spell the practice material that appears in the *Student Flip Book*. Students do not look at their flip books at this time. The pace of dictation should be brisk to help students establish a rhythm and overcome the tendency to focus on error-free entry. Do not pause at the end of these lines of dictated practice—line breaks occur because of page-width limitations rather than to guide the dictation. Careful observation and listening to your students' keystroking patterns will help you determine when to adjust the pace of dictation.

Independent Practice. At the conclusion of the teacher-dictated practice, direct students to open their *Student Flip Books* and enter the same practice lines independently, reading from the book. The *Flip Book* may hang from or be placed on top of the computer monitor, be placed between the keyboard and the computer or monitor, or be placed elsewhere on the desk area. In early lessons, you may find it useful to have the *Flip Book* somewhere between the monitor and the keyboard. This encourages students to check the monitor occasionally to ensure that they are typing the correct keys. It may also help them avoid or break the habit of looking at their fingers as they keyboard.

Bonus Practice. Bonus lessons immediately follow the regular practice exercises in the *Student Flip Book* for each lesson beginning with Lesson 6. They are a useful tool for students who need extra practice on certain keys or students who finish the regular practice early. They can also be used routinely to give the entire class extra practice if time permits.

Monitoring and Evaluating Students

Monitoring. Successful keyboarding teachers constantly walk around the classroom observing students and offering encouragement. This also provides an opportunity for modeling and reminding students of correct keyboarding techniques.

- **Speed Versus Accuracy.** Good techniques are the foundation upon which speed and accuracy are built. To develop keyboarding fluency, students need to balance their emphasis on accuracy and speed. Beginners need to be told that they will use their time more efficiently if they ignore errors while learning a new key. If students are concerned about errors, tell them to work on gaining speed with control. Encourage students to avoid looking at their fingers. Students will never learn touch typing if they are allowed to look at their fingers.

  Look for common error clusters. For example, errors on bottom-row letters, such as b, v, c, m, and n, may be due to sitting too close to the keyboard. Students may not have their bodies centered on the n key, their chairs may be too low, or they may need additional practice on keys on which they are error prone. Errors on top-row keys, such as p, q, and y, may be due to students sitting too far from the keyboard, resting their wrists on the keyboard, or locking their thumb under the keyboard.

  The periodic timed practice drills presented in *Keyboard Success* are designed to monitor student progress and enhance student motivation. Speed drills appear in Lessons 7, 16, 23, and 30. Their purpose is to help students develop a keyboarding speed equal to or greater than their handwriting rate. Based on results reported by teachers using *Keyboard Success,* it is reasonable to expect beginners to keyboard anywhere from 15 to 25 words per minute.

  The equipment your students are using and your preferred method of obtaining keyboarding rates from the timed drills will determine the accuracy and usefulness of this information.

If students are using equipment with which they can both save and print their practice drills (e.g., computers with access to printers), you can either check their saved files or have students print their timed practice drills and hand them in. If the equipment students are using will only print (e.g., an electric typewriter) or save (a portable keyboard), your choices are more limited. If the students are using equipment that neither prints nor saves, you will need to develop other methods for evaluating their keyboarding rates and accuracy.

The *Keyboard Success* script assumes that students will save their timed practice drills to a disk for you to check on screen or in printed form after the lesson. If the equipment students are using will not save or if you prefer to collect this information in another manner, you will need to change the instructions in the Keyboarding Rate sections of Lessons 7, 16, 23, and 30.

- **Gross Words A Minute (GWAM).** The standard formula for calculating GWAM is as follows:

$$\text{Keystroke} = \text{Letter, Punctuation, Space}$$
$$1 \text{ Word} = 5 \text{ Keystrokes}$$
$$\text{Total Keystrokes} \div 5 = \text{Total Words}$$
$$\text{Total Words} \div \text{Total Minutes} = \text{GWAM}$$

For ease of counting, the practice drills in *Keyboard Success* have been constructed on the basis of six-word lines; i.e., each full line typed equates to six typed words. A grid for recording handwriting and keyboarding rates and accuracy is provided in the Appendix. Also provided is a template for reporting GWAM results to your students.

Record the gross number of words typed in the first column of the Record Grid for Handwriting and Keyboarding Rates for each one-minute timed practice. To calculate the rate:
1. Count the total number of full lines typed during the 1-minute interval and multiply by 6.
2. Count the number of letters, spaces, and punctuation in any partially typed line and divide by 5.
3. Add these two numbers for the GWAM.

Record the number of words out of this total that are typed *correctly* in the next column.

Comparing the gross number of words typed with the number of words typed correctly, combined with classroom observation, should, over time, provide a measure of each student's progress in developing good keyboarding techniques.

Evaluating. It is not recommended that the timed exercises be used to grade students. Using the term "timed practice" may help to disassociate the timings from grading. If you are required to grade students, grade them on how well they demonstrate the techniques introduced and let them know what grading criteria you will use. A certificate of completion to be awarded to students when they complete all of the lessons in *Keyboard Success* is included in the Appendix.

Special Needs Students

In general, students who have the prerequisite motor skills and who can concentrate for a sustained period of time can successfully learn how to keyboard. When using the lessons in this program, make any adaptations necessary to accommodate students' individual needs. If necessary, work individually with the student during the lesson presentation and practice sessions, provide additional time, and repeat instructions as needed.

Teacher Enthusiasm

Students enjoy being taught by enthusiastic teachers. Try to convey a sense of excitement and enjoyment when teaching students keyboarding. Remember, keyboarding practice can often be tedious, so it's up to you not only to demonstrate correct technique but also to show enthusiasm for the subject and a caring attitude toward students.

Scope and Sequence

Skill Introduced	Lessons
Finger Naming	1–4
Keyboarding Position	1–2
Home Key Location	1–3
Key Introduction	2, 3, 5, 6, 8, 10, 12, 14, 15, 17, 19, 20, 22, 24, 26, 28, 29
Key Review Only	4, 9, 11, 13, 18, 21, 25, 27
Practice	2–30
Keyboarding Rate (Timed Practice)	7, 16, 23, 30

We hope you and your students will enjoy this journey to Keyboard Success!

Lesson 1

Introduction

Handwriting Rate
Finger Naming
Keyboarding Position
HOME Key Location

Materials

Keyboard Wall Chart
Keyboard Template
Handwriting Rate Worksheet
Finger Naming Worksheet
Position Chart for Good Keyboarding Habits
Record Grid for Handwriting and Keyboarding Rates

- *Duplicate the Handwriting Rate Worksheet and Finger Naming Worksheet from the Appendix. You will need one for each student.*

- *Display the Keyboard Wall Chart so that students can see it.*

Handwriting Rate

1 Today you begin the first of 30 keyboarding lessons. Entering information into a computer is called keyboarding. Before you begin keyboarding, I need some information about your handwriting rate. Your current handwriting rate will be compared to your keyboarding rate after you finish the last lesson. By then, you may be able to keyboard as fast as you write.

Distribute the Handwriting Rate Worksheet. A sample is shown at the right.

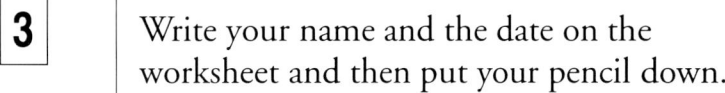

2 You should write as neatly and as quickly as you can. Place the Handwriting Rate Worksheet on your desk. Clear everything else away.

Pause and check.

3 Write your name and the date on the worksheet and then put your pencil down.

Pause and check.

4 When I say begin, write the three lines neatly one after another as many times as you can for 1 minute. Don't correct mistakes. You may write in cursive or print. Ready ... begin.

Check students, and say "stop" after 1 minute.

5 Now count the number of words you wrote. Write the number at the top of the worksheet.

Pause and check.

Collect student worksheets. Evaluate the legibility of each student's worksheet. Deduct points from the student's score for each illegible word. Enter each student's final score on the record grid found in the Appendix.

Lesson 1 • Finger Naming

The purpose of this exercise is to obtain baseline handwriting data for each student. This data should be recorded and compared to keyboarding data obtained after Lesson 30. A reasonable rate is for students to keyboard at a rate comparable to their handwriting rate.

Finger Naming

1 | Let's learn the names of our fingers.

2 | Watch me.

Face the class, right hand up, palm toward the class. Then make a fist.

3 | Your turn.

Demonstrate each behavior slowly. Pause and check.

4 | Raise your right hand.
Turn your palm toward me.
Make a fist.

5 | This is the pointer finger.
What finger?   [Student Response: *pointer finger*]
Raise your pointer finger. Leave it up.

Check.

6 | This is the middle finger.
What finger?   [Student Response: *middle finger*]
Raise your middle finger. Leave it up.

Check.
Repeat the procedure for the following fingers on the right hand: ring, little, thumb.

7 | Once more.

Check each action.

8 | Raise your right hand.
Turn your palm toward me.
Make a fist.

9 | Raise your little finger. Leave it up.
Raise your middle finger. Leave it up.
Raise your pointer finger. Leave it up.
Raise your ring finger. Leave it up.
Raise your thumb.
Put your right hand down.

Repeat the procedures in Steps 2–9 using the left hand.

Lesson 1 • Finger Naming

Distribute the Finger Naming Worksheet. A sample is shown at the right.

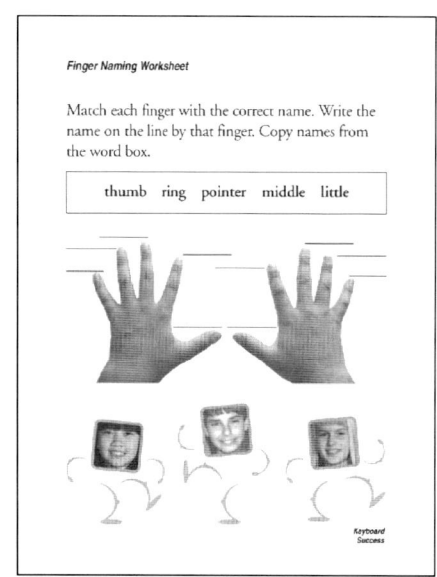

10 Look at your worksheet.
Match each finger with the correct name.
Write the name on the line by that finger.

11 As we go through the answers, check your worksheet.
Circle your errors and then correct them.

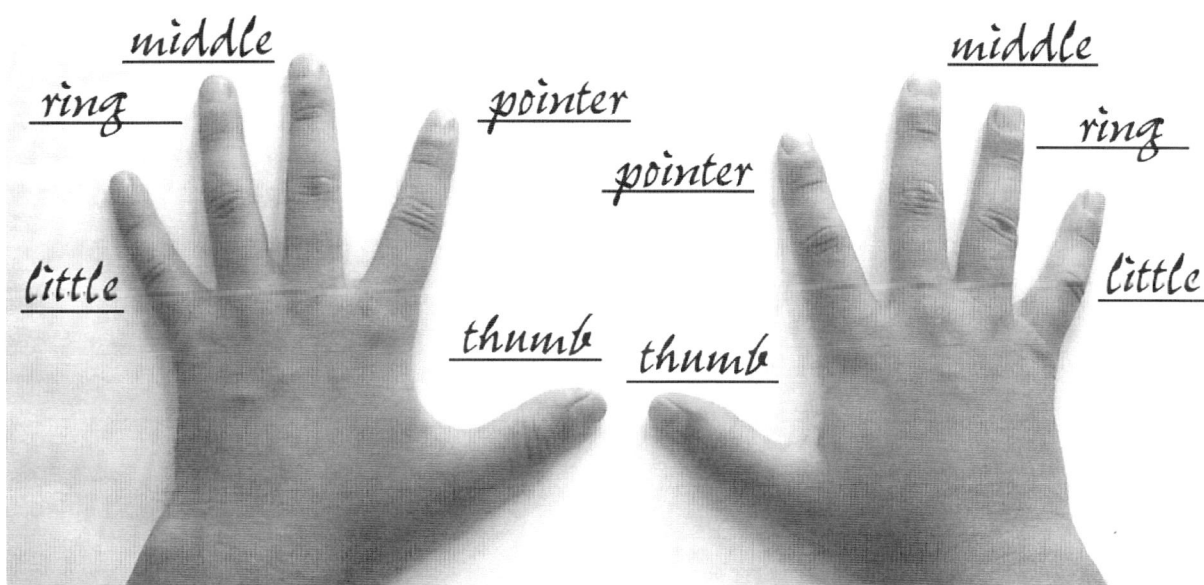

12 Little finger. Name it. [Student Response: *little*]
Ring finger. Name it. [Student Response: *ring*]
Middle finger. Name it. [Student Response: *middle*]

Repeat this procedure for each remaining finger.

Keyboard Success Teacher's Guide

Keyboarding Position

Use the following chart or the Wall Chart for reference for Steps 1–8. This chart also appears in Lesson 1 of the Student Flip Book and in the Appendix of this Teacher's Guide.

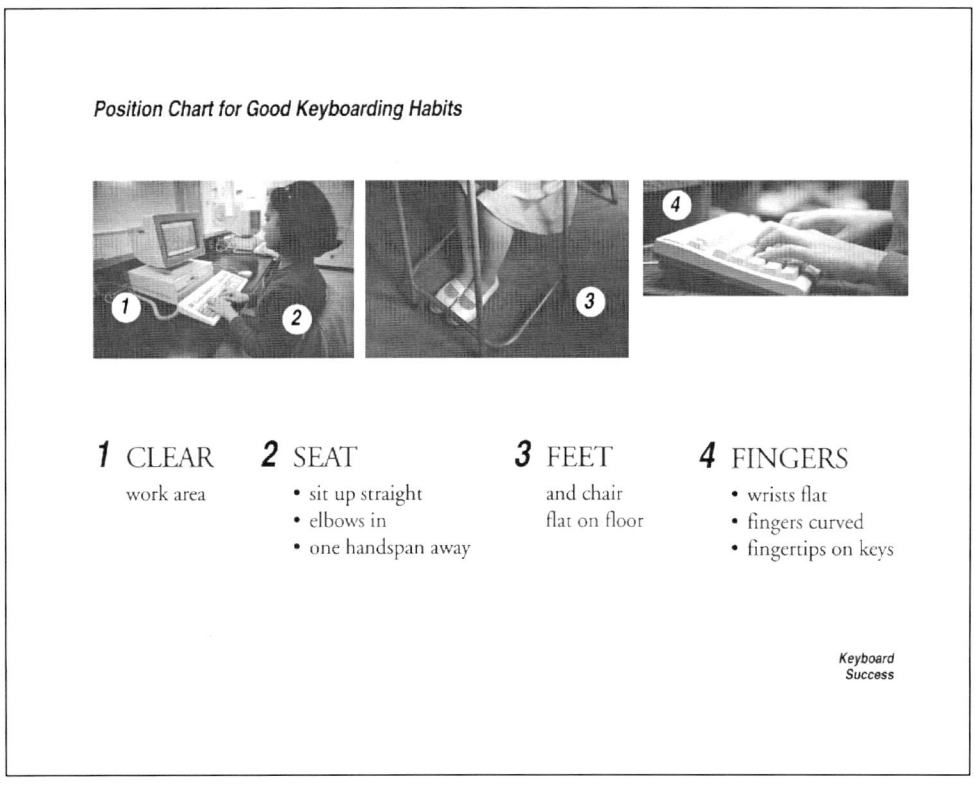

1 Turn to Lesson 1 in your *Flip Book*.

2 Entering information into a computer is called keyboarding. Before you begin keyboarding, you need to follow the rules on the Position Chart for Good Keyboarding Habits in Lesson 1 of your *Flip Book*. The *Wall Chart* also has cues to remind you of the correct position.

3 Touch the first picture.
Check to be sure your work area is clear.

Model this behavior.

Lesson 1 • Keyboarding Position

---

4   Sit up straight in your seat.
Hang your arms at your sides.
Now bend your elbows and bring your forearms up to the keyboard.

Model this behavior.

5   Now spread the fingers and thumb of your right hand as wide apart as you can, palm down.
Turn your hand sideways with your thumb pointing at your body.
Your body should be as far from the keyboard as your hand can stretch, or one handspan away.
Point your little finger toward the "j" key. This will center your body with the keyboard.

Model this behavior.

6   Keep your elbows in and lean forward slightly.

7   Touch the second picture.
Place your chair and feet flat on the floor. You may need to place your feet on the footrest beneath your desk.

Model this behavior.

8   Touch the third picture.
Extend your arms, keeping your wrists flat. Keep your fingers down and curved.
Now place your fingertips on the keyboard.
Your hands should follow the slant of the keyboard.

9 | Your turn. Practice each rule when I give the instruction.

Pause and check.

10 | Clear ... seat ... feet ... fingers.

Home Key Location

Point to the HOME keys on the keyboard on the Wall Chart. Each student should have a computer keyboard. If students do not have individual keyboards, distribute a copy of the Keyboard Template from the Appendix.

1 | These are called the HOME keys.
Always begin with your fingers on the HOME keys.

2 | I'll name the HOME keys you'll learn today.

Place the fingers of both your hands on the HOME keys on the Wall Chart.

3 | The keys for the left hand are: a ... s ... d ... f.

Touch each key on the Wall Chart.

4 | The HOME keys for the right hand are: SEMICOLON ... l ... k ... j.

Lesson 1 • Home Key Location

5 | I'll place my left-hand fingers on the HOME keys.

Place your left-hand fingers on the a-s-d-f keys. Then name each key.

6 | Your turn.
Place your left-hand fingers on these keys:
a ... s ... d ... f.

Check.

7 | I'll place my right-hand fingers next.

Place your right-hand fingers on the SEMICOLON-l-k-j keys.

8 | Your turn.
Place your right-hand fingers on these keys:
SEMICOLON ... l ... k ... j.

Check.

9 | Your fingers are now on the HOME keys.
What keys?   [Student Response: HOME *keys*]

End of Lesson 1

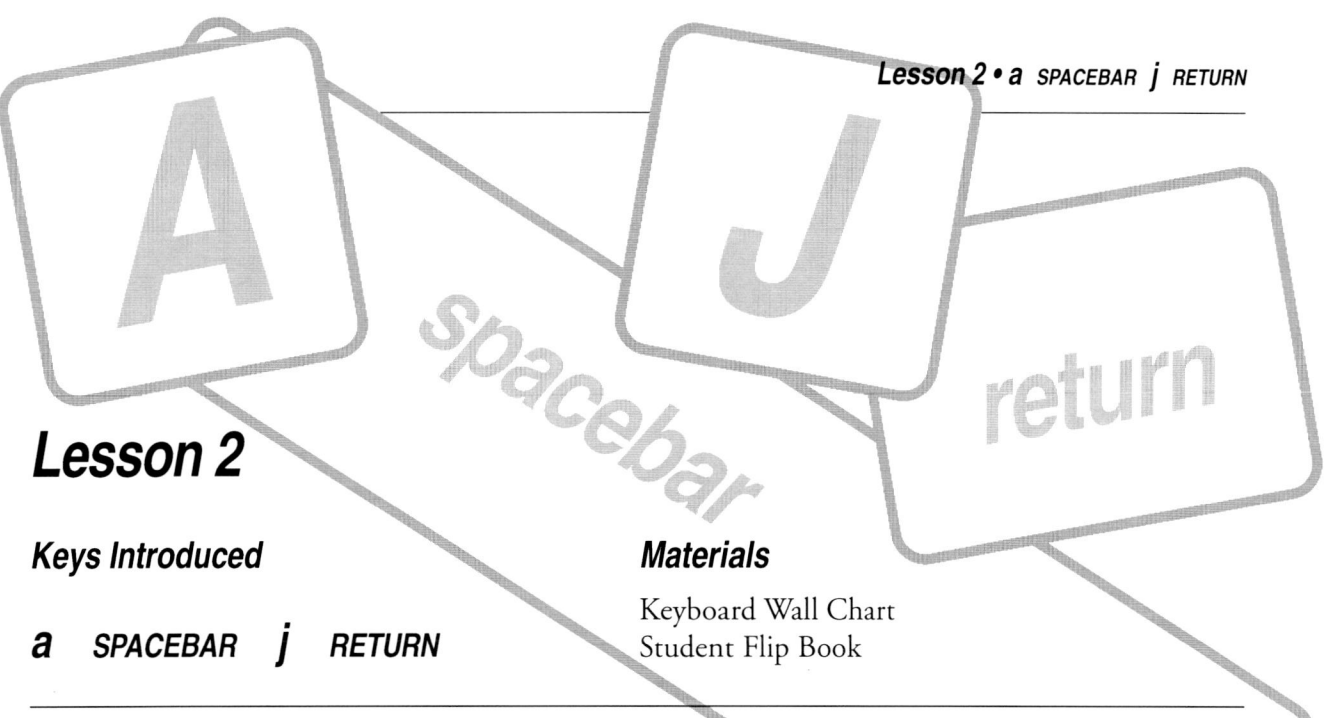

Lesson 2

Keys Introduced

a SPACEBAR j RETURN

Materials

Keyboard Wall Chart
Student Flip Book

Finger Naming Review

1 | Let's review the names of the fingers.

Check each action.

2 | Raise your right hand.
Turn your palm toward me.
Make a fist.

3 | Raise your little finger and leave it up.
Raise your pointer finger and leave it up.
Raise your middle finger and leave it up.
Raise your ring finger and leave it up.
Raise your thumb and leave it up.
Put your right hand down.

Repeat the procedure in Steps 2 and 3 using the left hand.

Keyboard Success Teacher's Guide

Keyboarding Position Review

1 | Let's review the rules for keyboarding.

2 | First, clear your work area.

Model this behavior.

3 | Sit up straight, elbows in, one handspan away.

Model this behavior.

4 | Feet and chair flat on the floor.

Model this behavior.

5 | Wrists flat, fingers down and curved, fingertips on the HOME keys.

6 | Your turn. Practice each rule when I give the instructions.

Pause and check.

7 | Clear … seat … feet … fingers.

Lesson 2 • a SPACEBAR *j* RETURN

Home Key Review

1 | I'll place my left-hand fingers on the HOME keys.

Place your fingers on the a-s-d-f keys on the Wall Chart.

2 | Your turn.
Place your left-hand fingers on these keys:
a ... s ... d ... f.

Check.

3 | I'll place my right-hand fingers next.

Place your fingers on the SEMICOLON-l-k-j keys on the Wall Chart.

4 | Your turn.
Place your right-hand fingers on these keys:
SEMICOLON ... l ... k ... j.

Check.

5 | Your fingers are now on the HOME keys.
What keys?   [Student Response: *HOME keys*]

Keyboard Success Teacher's Guide

Key Introduction: a SPACEBAR j RETURN

1 | Check your keyboarding position.

Pause and check.

2 | Clear ... seat ... feet ... fingers.

3 | Use your left-hand little finger to lightly tap the letter a.
Get ready.
Tap a ... a ... a.

Touch the SPACEBAR on the Wall Chart.

4 | This key is called the SPACEBAR.
The SPACEBAR lets you put a space on the line.
Use your right-hand thumb to tap the SPACEBAR.
Watch me tap the SPACEBAR with my right-hand thumb.

5 | Let's practice with SPACES.
Tap the SPACEBAR with your right-hand thumb.
aaa ... SPACE   aaa ... SPACE   aaa ... SPACE
aaa ... SPACE   aaa ...SPACE   aaa ... SPACE

6 | Use your right-hand pointer finger to lightly tap j.
Get ready.
Tap j ... j ... j.

Lesson 2 • a SPACEBAR j RETURN

7 | Let's practice with SPACES.
Tap the SPACEBAR with your right-hand thumb.

| jjj …SPACE | jjj … SPACE | jjj … SPACE |
| jjj …SPACE | jjj … SPACE | jjj … SPACE |

8 | Let's practice with both keys.
Get ready.

9 |

aaa … SPACE	jjj … SPACE	jaj … SPACE	aja …SPACE
aaa … SPACE	jjj … SPACE	aja … SPACE	jaj … SPACE
aja … SPACE	jaj … SPACE	jja … SPACE	aaj … SPACE
jja … SPACE	aaj …SPACE	jaj … SPACE	aja … SPACE
aja … SPACE	jaj … SPACE	jja … SPACE	aaj …SPACE

Touch RETURN on the Wall Chart.

10 | This key is called RETURN.
RETURN lets you work on a new line.
Place your fingers on the HOME keys.
Look at your right hand.
Reach over and tap RETURN with your right-hand little finger.

11 | Let's practice with RETURN.
Tap RETURN with your right-hand little finger.

| aj … RETURN | ja … RETURN | jaj … RETURN | aaj … RETURN |

Practice

1 | Listen: a-a-a
You will enter letters on your keyboard as I spell them.
Get ready.

Spell each group of letters in Step 2.
Pause and say "SPACE" when appropriate.
Say "RETURN" at the end of the line.
Adjust dictation rate to the students' skill level.

2 | aaa jjj aaa jjj aaa jjj aj aj ja ja a ja
ja ja ja aj aj aj a ja a ja jaa jaa jaj jaj
jaa jaa jaa ajj ajj ajj jaj jaj jaj aja aja

3 | Open your *Flip Book* to Lesson 2.
Enter each line twice.
Tap RETURN at the end of each line.
Try not to look at your fingers.
Don't correct mistakes.
You may begin.

Monitor the class for correct keyboarding position:
- ☑ *One handspan away from the keyboard, feet flat on the floor.*
- ☑ *Fingers curved over the HOME keys.*
- ☑ *Hands still.*
- ☑ *Quick, snappy keystrokes.*

End of Lesson 2

Lesson 3

Keys Introduced

s   k

Materials

Keyboard Wall Chart
Student Flip Book

Finger Naming Review

1 | Let's review the names of the fingers.

Check each action.

2 | Raise your right hand.
Turn your palm toward me.
Make a fist.

3 | Raise your little finger and leave it up.
Raise your ring finger and leave it up.
Raise your middle finger and leave it up.
Raise your pointer finger and leave it up.
Raise your thumb and leave it up.
Put your right hand down.

Repeat the procedure in Steps 2 and 3 using the left hand.

Keyboard Success Teacher's Guide

Key Review

| 1 | Check your keyboarding position on the HOME keys. |

Pause and check.

| 2 | Clear ... seat ... feet ... fingers. |

| 3 | Let's review.
Remember to tap the keys lightly.
Get ready. |

| 4 | aaa ... SPACE   aaa ... SPACE   jjj ... SPACE   aaa ... SPACE
jjj ... SPACE   aaa ... SPACE   aaa ... SPACE   jjj ... SPACE
aaa ... SPACE   jjj ... SPACE   aaa ... SPACE   jjj ... SPACE
aaj ... SPACE   jja ... SPACE   aja ... SPACE   ajj ... SPACE
aaa ... SPACE   jjj ... SPACE   ajj ... SPACE   jaj ... SPACE |

Key Introduction: s k

| 1 | Check your keyboarding position on the HOME keys. |

Pause and check.

| 2 | Clear ... seat ... feet ... fingers. |

Lesson 3 • s k

3 You're going to learn two new keys.
Here's the s on the keyboard.

Touch the key on the Wall Chart.

4 Use your left-hand ring finger.
Watch me tap s.

5 Get ready.

Instruct students in a rhythmic manner.

6 Tap s ... s ... s.

7 Let's practice with SPACES.

| sss ... SPACE | sss ... SPACE | sss ... SPACE | sss ... SPACE |
| sss ... SPACE | sss ... SPACE | sss ... SPACE | sss ... SPACE |

8 Now let's learn k.
Here's k on the keyboard.

Touch the key on the Wall Chart.

9 Use your right-hand middle finger.
Watch me tap k.

Keyboard Success Teacher's Guide

10 | Get ready.

Instruct students in a rhythmic manner.

11 | Tap k ... k ... k.

12 | Let's practice with SPACES.
| kkk ... SPACE | kkk ... SPACE | kkk ... SPACE | kkk ... SPACE |
| kkk ... SPACE | kkk ... SPACE | kkk ... SPACE | kkk ... SPACE |

13 | Let's practice with both keys.
Get ready.

14 |
sss ... SPACE	sss ... SPACE	kkk ... SPACE	kkk ... SPACE
sss ... SPACE	kkk ... SPACE	sas ... SPACE	sas ... SPACE
kjk ... SPACE	kjk ... SPACE	sks ... SPACE	ksk ... SPACE
aks ... SPACE	aks ... SPACE	sas ... SPACE	aks ... SPACE

Lesson 3 • s k

Practice

1 Listen: j-a-k
You will enter letters as I say them.
Get ready.

Spell each group of letters in Step 2.
Pause and say "SPACE" when appropriate.
Say "RETURN" at the end of the line.
Adjust dictation rate to the students' skill level.

2 jak a jaks sak sks aks aka ksk jka jaj
sass jak ask a sak as a ask a as a ask a
kass asks ask kass jask sass kass jass

3 Open your *Flip Book* to Lesson 3.
Enter each line twice.
Tap RETURN at the end of each line.
Try not to look at your fingers.
Don't correct mistakes.
You may begin.

Monitor the class for correct keyboarding position:
☑ *One handspan away from the keyboard, feet flat on the floor.*
☑ *Fingers curved over the HOME keys.*
☑ *Hands still.*
☑ *Quick, snappy keystrokes.*

End of Lesson 3

Lesson 4

Review

Materials

Student Flip Book

Finger Naming Review

* *Do not use any visual prompts for finger names during this lesson.*

| 1 | Let's review the names of the fingers. |

Check each action.

| 2 | Raise your right hand.
Turn your palm toward me.
Make a fist. |

| 3 | Raise your little finger and leave it up.
Raise your thumb and leave it up.
Raise your middle finger and leave it up.
Raise your pointer finger and leave it up.
Raise your ring finger and leave it up.
Put your right hand down. |

Repeat the procedure in Steps 2 and 3 using the left hand.

Key Review

1 Check your keyboarding position.

Pause and check.

2 Clear ... seat ... feet ... fingers.

3 Let's review.
Get ready.

4
aaa ... SPACE	jjj ... SPACE	sss ... SPACE	kkk ... SPACE
jjj ... SPACE	jsj ... SPACE	jkj ... SPACE	skj ... SPACE
akj ... SPACE	aka ... SPACE	sak ... SPACE	saj ... SPACE
kak ... SPACE	ska ... SPACE	kss ... SPACE	jak ... SPACE

Lesson 4 • Finger Naming and Key Review

Practice

1   Listen: ask
You will enter letters as I say them.
Get ready.

Say and spell each word or group of letters in Step 2.
Pause and say "SPACE" when appropriate.
Say "RETURN" at the end of the line.
Adjust dictation rate to the students' skill level.

2   ask a as a ask a as a sak a sak kak
sass kas sass jass kass kjk ksk kak
ak ak jak jak sak sak ask ak ask kass

3   Open your *Flip Book* to Lesson 4.
Enter each line twice.
Tap RETURN at the end of each line.
Don't correct mistakes.
You may begin.

Monitor the class for correct keyboarding position:
☑ *One handspan away from the keyboard, feet flat on the floor.*
☑ *Fingers curved over the HOME keys.*
☑ *Hands still.*
☑ *Quick, snappy keystrokes.*

End of Lesson 4

Lesson 5 • d l

Lesson 5

Keys Introduced

d l

Materials

Keyboard Wall Chart
Student Flip Book

Key Review

1 | Check your keyboarding position.

Pause and check.

2 | Clear ... seat ... feet ... fingers.

3 | Let's review.
Get ready.

4 |
jjj ... SPACE   sss ... SPACE   kkk ... SPACE   aaa ... SPACE
jjj ... SPACE   jjj ... SPACE   aka ... SPACE   skj ... SPACE
kka ... SPACE   aak ... SPACE   jjs ... SPACE   jkj ... SPACE
ksa ... SPACE   sks ... SPACE   jas ... SPACE   kks ... SPACE

Key Introduction: d l

| 1 | Check your keyboarding position. |

Pause and check.

| 2 | Clear ... seat ... feet ... fingers. |

| 3 | You're going to learn two new keys.
Here's d on the keyboard. |

Touch the key on the Wall Chart.

| 4 | Use your left-hand middle finger to tap d.
Watch me tap d. |

| 5 | Get ready.
Tap d ... d ... d. |

| 6 | Let's practice. |

| 7 | Tap the SPACEBAR with your right thumb.
ddd ... SPACE   ddd ... SPACE   ddd ... SPACE   ddd ... SPACE
ddd ... SPACE   ddd ... SPACE   ddd ... SPACE   ddd ... SPACE |

Lesson 5 • d l

8 Here's l on the keyboard.

Touch the key on the Wall Chart.

9 Use your right-hand ring finger to tap l.
Watch me tap l.

10 Get ready.
Tap l … l … l.

11 Let's practice.
Tap the SPACEBAR with your right-hand thumb.

| lll … SPACE | lll … SPACE | lll … SPACE | lll … SPACE |
| lll … SPACE | lll … SPACE | lll … SPACE | lll … SPACE |

12 Let's practice with both keys.
Get ready.

13

ddd … SPACE	ddd … SPACE	lll … SPACE	lll … SPACE
dld … SPACE	dld … SPACE	ldl … SPACE	ldl … SPACE
dld … SPACE	dld … SPACE	dld … SPACE	dld … SPACE

Practice

1 Listen: lass
You will enter letters as I say them.
Get ready.

Say and spell each word in Step 2.
Pause and say "SPACE" when appropriate.
Say "RETURN" at the end of the line.
Adjust dictation rate to the students' skill level.

2 lass adds a salsa salad a sad dad
alas a dallas a sad kass ads a lad adds
ask lads ask a lass all dads add salsa

3 Open your *Flip Book* to Lesson 5.
Enter each line twice.
Tap RETURN at the end of each line.
Don't correct mistakes.
You may begin.

Monitor the class for correct keyboarding position:
☑ *One handspan away from the keyboard, feet flat on the floor.*
☑ *Fingers curved over the HOME keys.*
☑ *Hands still.*
☑ *Quick, snappy keystrokes.*

End of Lesson 5

Lesson 6 • SEMICOLON f

Lesson 6

Keys Introduced

SEMICOLON *f*

Materials

Keyboard Wall Chart
Student Flip Book

Key Review

| 1 | Check your keyboarding position. |

Pause and check.

| 2 | Clear ... seat ... feet ... fingers. |

| 3 | Let's review.
Get ready. |

| 4 | ddd ... SPACE   lll ... SPACE   ddd ... SPACE   sss ... SPACE
kkk ... SPACE   dkd ... SPACE   ldl ... SPACE   sll ... SPACE
kak ... SPACE   dda ... SPACE   sll ... SPACE   aad ... SPACE
ldl ... SPACE   sks ... SPACE   ksk ... SPACE   dsa ... SPACE |

41

Key Introduction: SEMICOLON f

1 Check your keyboarding position.

Pause and check.

2 Clear ... seat ... feet ... fingers.

3 You're going to learn two new keys.
Here's SEMICOLON on the keyboard.

Touch the key on the Wall Chart.

4 Use your right-hand little finger to tap SEMICOLON.
Watch me tap SEMICOLON.

5 Get ready.

Instruct students in a rhythmic manner.

6 Tap SEMICOLON ... SEMICOLON ... SEMICOLON.

7 Let's practice with SPACES.
Tap the SPACEBAR with your right thumb.
Get ready.

;;; ... SPACE   ;;; ... SPACE   ;;; ... SPACE   ;;; ... SPACE
;;; ... SPACE   ;;; ... SPACE   ;;; ... SPACE   ;;; ... SPACE

Lesson 6 • SEMICOLON f

8 | Now let's learn f.

Touch the key on the Wall Chart.

9 | Use your left-hand pointer finger to tap f.
Watch me tap f.

10 | Get ready.

Instruct students in a rhythmic manner.

11 | Tap f … f … f.

12 | Let's practice with SPACES.

fff … SPACE	fff … SPACE	fff … SPACE	fff … SPACE
fff … SPACE	fff … SPACE	fff … SPACE	fff … SPACE

13 | Let's practice with both keys.
Get ready.

14 |

;;; … SPACE	;;; … SPACE	;;; … SPACE	;;; … SPACE
;;; … SPACE	;;; … SPACE	fff … SPACE	fff … SPACE
fff … SPACE	fff … SPACE	fff … SPACE	fff … SPACE
;l; … SPACE	;l; … SPACE	fdf … SPACE	fdf … SPACE
fsd … SPACE	;lk … SPACE	dsf … SPACE	dfd … SPACE

Keyboard Success Teacher's Guide

Practice

1   Listen: ask dad;
You will enter words as I spell them.
Get ready.

Say and spell each word in Step 2.
Pause and say "SPACE" when appropriate.
Say "RETURN" at the end of the line.
Adjust dictation rate to the students' skill level.

2   ask dad; ask a lass; dads salads; ads;
a fall fad; a flask falls; fall flasks;
ask all lads; dads fads; salad fads;

3   Open your *Flip Book* to Lesson 6.
Enter each line twice.
Tap RETURN at the end of each line.
Don't correct mistakes.
When you finish, enter each line in Bonus Lesson 6 twice. Bonus Lesson 6 is on the next page in your *Flip Book*.
You may begin.

Monitor the class for correct keyboarding position:
☑ *One handspan away from the keyboard, feet flat on the floor.*
☑ *Fingers curved over the HOME keys.*
☑ *Hands still.*
☑ *Quick, snappy keystrokes.*

End of Lesson 6

Lesson 7 • Review and Timed Practice

Lesson 7

Review and Timed Practice

Materials

Watch/clock with a second hand
Student Flip Book

Key Review

1 | Check your keyboarding position.

Pause and check.

2 | Clear ... seat ... feet ... fingers.

3 | Let's review.
Get ready.

4 |

;;; ... SPACE	fff ... SPACE	;;; ... SPACE	fff ... SPACE
ddd ... SPACE	lll ... SPACE	dll ... SPACE	dll ... SPACE
;l; ... SPACE	fdf ... SPACE	flf ... SPACE	d;d ... SPACE
;l; ... SPACE	ldd ... SPACE	dll ... SPACE	l;; ... SPACE
l;l ... SPACE	dff ... SPACE	f;f ... SPACE	ldl ... SPACE

Keyboard Success Teacher's Guide

Practice

1 Listen: ask dad;
You will enter words as I spell them.
Get ready.

Say and spell each word in Step 2.
Pause and say "SPACE" when appropriate.
Say "RETURN" at the end of the line.
Adjust dictation rate to the students' skill level.

2 ask dad; ask a lass; a lads salal salad;
fall flasks; fall fads fall; a fall fad;
a sad lass falls; alas a lad; salad fads;

3 Open your *Flip Book* to Lesson 7.
Enter each line twice.
Tap RETURN at the end of each line.
Don't correct mistakes.
When you finish, enter each line in Bonus Lesson 7 twice.
You may begin.

Monitor the class for correct keyboarding position:
☑ *One handspan away from the keyboard, feet flat on the floor.*
☑ *Fingers curved over the HOME keys.*
☑ *Hands still.*
☑ *Quick, snappy keystrokes.*

Lesson 7 • Review and Timed Practice

Keyboarding Rate

- *This lesson includes timed practice for keys introduced in Lessons 2–6. The purpose of this exercise is to determine each student's baseline keyboarding rate. To accurately measure students' progress in the program, it is important to obtain this data.*

- *You will need a watch or clock with a second hand.*

- *Important Note: The following script assumes that students will save their timed practice drills to a disk for you to check on screen or in printed form after the lesson. If the equipment students are using will not save files or if you prefer to collect this information in another manner, you will need to adjust the following instructions.*

| 1 | You're going to practice keyboarding as quickly and accurately as you can for 1 minute. You won't be graded, but I will compare your keyboarding speed with your handwriting speed, so type quickly but carefully. |

| 2 | Look at Bonus Lesson 7 again. |

Check.

| 3 | Touch the group of three lines. |

Check.

Keyboard Success Teacher's Guide

4 When I say begin, type the three lines one after the other as many times as you can.
Tap RETURN at the end of each line.
Try not to look at your fingers.
Don't correct mistakes.
I will stop you after 1 minute.

5 Check your keyboarding position.

Pause.

6 Ready ... begin.

Allow 1 minute.

7 Stop.

Have students save their timed keyboarding work to a disk to hand in.

8 Now save your work to your disk and leave the disk with me.

After the lesson, review the students' work, either on screen or in printed form, for speed and accuracy.

Calculating Gross Words A Minute (GWAM)

1 Count the total number of full lines typed during the 1-minute interval and place on Line A.

Multiply the number of lines by 6 to obtain a preliminary word count. (Each line contains the equivalent of 6 words or 30 characters.) Place on Line B.

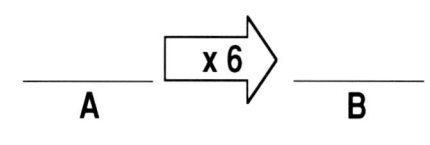

2 Count the number of letters, punctuation marks, and spaces in a partially typed line. Place on Line C.

Divide the number of characters by 5 to calculate the number of words in the partially typed line. Place on Line D.

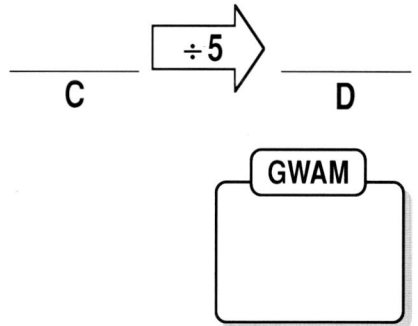

3 Add Lines B & D to obtain student's GWAM.

Record this number in the first column for Lesson 7 on the Record Grid for Handwriting and Keyboarding Rates.

In the second column of the Record Grid, record the total number of words typed without error.

You may wish to provide students with a written report for each timed practice. A template for this purpose is provided in the Appendix. Copy and complete one form for each student.

End of Lesson 7

Lesson 8 • e h

Lesson 8

Keys Introduced

e   h

Materials

Keyboard Wall Chart
Student Flip Book

Key Review

1 | Check your keyboarding position.

Pause and check.

2 | Clear ... seat ... feet ... fingers.

3 | Let's review.
Get ready.

4 |
fff ... SPACE	ddd ... SPACE	jjj ... SPACE	kkk ... SPACE
sss ... SPACE	lll ... SPACE	;;; ... SPACE	daf ... SPACE
lak ... SPACE	jdj ... SPACE	alk ... SPACE	lk; ... SPACE
as ... SPACE	as ... SPACE	ls ... SPACE	ls ... SPACE
faf ... SPACE	lal; ... SPACE	kak ... SPACE	jlj; ... SPACE
dsd ... SPACE	lsl; ... SPACE	sasa ... SPACE	lalj ... SPACE

51

Keyboard Success Teacher's Guide

Key Introduction: e h

| 1 | Check your keyboarding position. |

Pause and check.

| 2 | Clear ... seat ... feet ... fingers. |

| 3 | You're going to learn two new keys.
Here's e on the keyboard. |

Touch the key on the Wall Chart.

| 4 | Use your left-hand middle finger.
Watch me reach up and tap e.
When you reach for a key, keep your other fingers on the HOME keys.
This is called anchoring. |

| 5 | Get ready. |

Instruct students in a rhythmic manner.

| 6 | Tap e ... HOME ... e ... HOME ... e ... HOME. |

| 7 | Let's practice with SPACES. Anchor the fingers you're not using.
eee ... HOME ... SPACE   eee ... HOME ... SPACE   eee ... HOME ... SPACE
ded ... SPACE   ded ... SPACE   ded ... SPACE
ded ... SPACE   ded ... SPACE   ded ... SPACE |

Lesson 8 • e h

8 | Now let's learn h.

Touch the key on the Wall Chart.

9 | Use your right-hand pointer finger.
Watch me reach over and tap h.

10 | Get ready.

Instruct students in a rhythmic manner.

11 | Tap h … HOME … h … HOME … h … HOME.

12 | Let's practice with spaces.
Anchor the fingers you're not using.
hhh … HOME … SPACE	hhh … HOME … SPACE	hhh … HOME … SPACE
jhj … SPACE	jhj … SPACE	jhj … SPACE
jhj … SPACE	jhj … SPACE	jhj … SPACE

13 | Let's practice with both keys.
Get ready.

14 |
eee … HOME … SPACE	eee … HOME … SPACE	eee … HOME … SPACE
ded … SPACE	ded … SPACE	ded … SPACE
ded … SPACE	ded … SPACE	ded … SPACE
hhh … HOME … SPACE	hhh … HOME … SPACE	hhh … HOME … SPACE
jhj … SPACE	jhj … SPACE	jhj … SPACE
jhj … SPACE	jhj … SPACE	jhj … SPACE
dee … HOME … SPACE	jhh … HOME … SPACE	dee … HOME … SPACE

Practice

1 Listen: dad led elks;
You will enter words as I spell them.
Get ready.

Say and spell each word in Step 2.
Pause and say "SPACE" when appropriate.
Say "RETURN" at the end of the line.
Adjust dictation rate to the students' skill level.

2 dad led elks; feed eels leeks; seals fade;
he had; held half; has a heel; she heals;
seal a flask; as she ladles; dead ahead;

3 Open your *Flip Book* to Lesson 8.
Enter each line twice.
Tap RETURN at the end of each line.
Don't correct mistakes.
When you finish, type each line in Bonus Lesson 8 twice.
You may begin.

Monitor the class for correct keyboarding position:
☑ *One handspan away from the keyboard, feet flat on the floor.*
☑ *Fingers curved over the HOME keys.*
☑ *Hands still.*
☑ *Quick, snappy keystrokes.*

End of Lesson 8

Lesson 9

Review

Materials

Student Flip Book

Key Review

1 Check your keyboarding position.

Pause and check.

2 Clear ... seat ... feet ... fingers.

3 Let's review.
Get ready.

4
aaa ... SPACE	jjj ... SPACE	sss ... SPACE	lll ... SPACE
eee ... HOME ... SPACE	;;; ... SPACE	hhh ... HOME ... SPACE
fff ... SPACE	kkk ... SPACE	ddd ... SPACE	ded ... SPACE
ded ... SPACE	fas ... SPACE	jhj ... SPACE	jhj ... SPACE
klf ... SPACE	klf ... SPACE	as ... SPACE	as ... SPACE
lel ... SPACE	lel ... SPACE	hee ... HOME ... SPACE
ehh ... HOME ... SPACE		ehh ... HOME ... SPACE

Practice

1
Listen: elks seek;
You will enter words as I spell them.
Get ready.

Say and spell each word in Step 2.
Pause and say "SPACE" when appropriate.
Say "RETURN" at the end of the line.
Adjust dictation rate to the students' skill level.

2
elks seek; seals feed; a fake dead eel;
ha ha hee hee; seek shade; sea shells;
she had asked; safe lakes; a half fed elf;

3
Open your *Flip Book* to Lesson 9.
Enter each line twice.
Tap RETURN at the end of each line.
Don't correct mistakes.
Remember to anchor the fingers you're not using.
When you finish, type each line in Bonus Lesson 9 twice.
You may begin.

Monitor the class for correct keyboarding position:
- ☑ *Wrists flat, elbows in, eyes on copy.*
- ☑ *Correct reach, anchoring, and return HOME.*
- ☑ *Steady rhythm, correct use of SPACEBAR and RETURN.*

End of Lesson 9

Lesson 10 • o r

Lesson 10

Keys Introduced

o   r

Materials

Keyboard Wall Chart
Student Flip Book

Key Review

1 | Check your keyboarding position.

Pause and check.

2 | Clear ... seat ... feet ... fingers.

3 | Let's review.
Get ready.

4 | eee ... HOME ... SPACE   hhh ... HOME ... SPACE   eee ... HOME ... SPACE
hhh ... SPACE   ;;; ... SPACE   fff ... SPACE   eee ... HOME ... SPACE
hhh ... HOME ... SPACE   ded ... SPACE   jhj ... SPACE   ded ... SPACE
jhj ... SPACE   ded ... SPACE   jhj ... SPACE   ded ... SPACE
jhj ... SPACE   dee ... HOME ... SPACE   hee ... HOME ... SPACE
fee ... HOME ... SPACE   ded ... SPACE   jhj ... SPACE

Keyboard Success Teacher's Guide

Key Introduction: o r

1 | Check your keyboarding position.

Pause and check.

2 | Clear ... seat ... feet ... fingers.

3 | You're going to learn two new keys.
Here's o on the keyboard.

Touch the key on the Wall Chart.

4 | Use your right-hand ring finger.
Watch me reach up, tap o, and return HOME.

5 | Get ready.

Instruct students in a rhythmic manner.

6 | Tap o ... HOME ... o ... HOME ... o ... HOME.

7 | Let's practice with SPACES.
Anchor the fingers you're not using.
ooo ... HOME ... SPACE   ooo ... HOME ... SPACE   ooo ... HOME ... SPACE
lol ... SPACE   lol ... SPACE   lol ... SPACE   lol ... SPACE
lol ... SPACE   lol ... SPACE   lol ... SPACE   lol ... SPACE

Lesson 10 • o r

8 | Now let's learn r.

Touch the key on the Wall Chart.

9 | Use your left-hand pointer finger.
Watch me reach up, tap r, and return HOME.

10 | Get ready.

Instruct students in a rhythmic manner.

11 | Tap r ... HOME ... r ... HOME ... r ... HOME.

12 | Let's practice with SPACES.
Anchor the fingers you're not using.
rrr ... HOME ... SPACE   rrr ... HOME ... SPACE   rrr ... HOME ... SPACE
frf ... SPACE   frf ... SPACE   frf ... SPACE   frf ... SPACE
frf ... SPACE   frf ... SPACE   frf ... SPACE   frf ... SPACE

13 | Let's practice with both keys.
Get ready.

14 | ooo ... HOME ... SPACE   ooo ... HOME ... SPACE   ooo ... HOME ... SPACE
lol ... SPACE   lol ... SPACE   lol ... SPACE   lol ... SPACE
lol ... SPACE   lol ... SPACE   lol ... SPACE   lol ... SPACE

15

rrr ... HOME ... SPACE	rrr ... HOME ... SPACE	rrr ... HOME ... SPACE
frf ... SPACE	frf ... SPACE	frf ... SPACE	frf ... SPACE
frf ... SPACE	frf ... SPACE	frf ... SPACE	lol ... SPACE
lol ... SPACE	frf ... SPACE	frf ... SPACE	lol ... SPACE

Practice

1 Listen: old fool;
You will enter words as I spell them.
Get ready.

Say and spell each word in Step 2.
Pause and say "SPACE" when appropriate.
Say "RETURN" at the end of the line.
Adjust dictation rate to the students' skill level.

2 old fool; hello floor; look offshore;
red rose; share her doll; real red rakes;
look for food; reorder jars; old hoses;

3 Open your *Flip Book* to Lesson 10.
Enter each line twice.
Tap RETURN at the end of each line.
Don't correct mistakes.
When you finish, type each line in Bonus Lesson 10 twice.
You may begin.

Monitor the class for correct keyboarding position:
☑ *Wrists flat, elbows in, eyes on copy.*
☑ *Correct reach, anchoring, and return HOME.*
☑ *Steady rhythm, correct use of SPACEBAR and RETURN.*

End of Lesson 10

Lesson 11

Review

Materials

Student Flip Book

Key Review

1 | Check your keyboarding position.

Pause and check.

2 | Clear ... seat ... feet ... fingers.

3 | Let's review.
Get ready.

Say "SPACE" when appropriate.

4 |

ooo ... HOME	rrr ... HOME	hhh ... HOME	rrr ... HOME
eee ... HOME	ooo ... HOME	rrr ... HOME	eee ... HOME
lol frf	lol frf	ded jhj	jhj ded
loo ... HOME	foo ... HOME	lee ... HOME	hoo ... HOME
ree ... HOME	loo ... HOME	hee ... HOME	foo ... HOME
jhl frd	lok frd	llo ... HOME	llo ... HOME

Keyboard Success Teacher's Guide

Practice

1 Listen: old jello;
You will enter words as I spell them.
Get ready.

Say and spell each word in Step 2.
Pause and say "SPACE" when appropriate.
Say "RETURN" at the end of the line.
Adjust dictation rate to the students' skill level.

2 old jello; fool a horse; old hoses; hello;
real red roses; ears hear larks; sold food;
look for rolls; dark lakes; order shoes;

3 Open your *Flip Book* to Lesson 11.
Enter each line twice.
Tap RETURN at the end of each line.
Don't correct mistakes.
When you finish, type each line in Bonus Lesson 11 twice.
You may begin.

Monitor the class for correct keyboarding position:
☑ *Wrists flat, elbows in, eyes on copy.*
☑ *Correct reach, anchoring, and return HOME.*
☑ *Steady rhythm, correct use of SPACEBAR and RETURN.*

End of Lesson 11

Lesson 12 • i t

Lesson 12

Keys Introduced

i   *t*

Materials

Keyboard Wall Chart
Student Flip Book

Key Review

1 | Check your keyboarding position.

Pause and check.

2 | Clear ... seat ... feet ... fingers.

3 | Let's review.
Get ready.

4 |
eee ... HOME	hhh ... HOME	ooo ... HOME	rrr ... HOME
eee ... HOME	ooo ... HOME	hhh ... HOME	rrr ... HOME
frf frf	jhj jhj	ded ded	lol lol
asa asa;	ror ... HOME	ror ... HOME	or ... HOME
jhj jhj;	l;l l;l	jhj l;l	frf frf
ror ... HOME	hjh ... HOME	oor ... HOME	hjh ... HOME

63

Keyboard Success Teacher's Guide

Key Introduction: i t

| **1** | Check your keyboarding position. |

Pause and check.

| **2** | Clear ... seat ... feet ... fingers. |

| **3** | You're going to learn two new keys.
Here's i on the keyboard. |

Touch the key on the Wall Chart.

| **4** | Use your right-hand middle finger.
Watch me reach up, tap i, and return HOME. |

| **5** | Get ready. |

Instruct students in a rhythmic manner.

| **6** | Tap i ... HOME ... i ... HOME ... i ... HOME. |

| **7** | Let's practice with spaces.
Anchor the fingers you're not using.
iii ... HOME   iii ... HOME   iii ... HOME   iii ... HOME
iii ... HOME   iii ... HOME   iii ... HOME   iii ... HOME
kik   kik   kik   kik   kik   kik   kik   kik |

Lesson 12 • i t

8 | Now let's learn t.

Touch the key on the Wall Chart.

9 | Use your left-hand pointer finger.
Watch me reach up, tap t, and return HOME.

10 | Get ready.

Instruct students in a rhythmic manner.

11 | Tap t ... HOME ... t ... HOME ... t ... HOME.

12 | Let's practice with SPACES.
Anchor the fingers you're not using.

ttt ... HOME	ttt ... HOME	ttt ... HOME	ttt ... HOME
ttt ... HOME	ttt ... HOME	ttt ... HOME	ttt ... HOME
ftf ftf	ftf ftf	ftf ftf	ftf ftf

13 | Let's practice with both new keys.
Get ready.

14 |

iii ... HOME	iii ... HOME	iii ... HOME	iii ... HOME
iii ... HOME	iii ... HOME	iii ... HOME	iii ... HOME
kik kik	kik kik	kik kik	kik kik
ttt ... HOME	ttt ... HOME	ttt ... HOME	ttt ... HOME
ttt ... HOME	ttt ... HOME	ttt ... HOME	ttt ... HOME
ftf ftf	ftf ftf	ftf ftf	ftf ftf
kik ftf	ftf kik	ftf kik	kik ftf

Practice

1
Listen: if it is;
You will enter words as I spell them.
Get ready.

Say and spell each word in Step 2.
Pause and say "SPACE" when appropriate.
Say "RETURN" at the end of the line.
Adjust dictation rate to the students' skill level.

2
if it is; like to ride; the kite flies;
a toad tried; ate it at first; hire kids;
take to the trail; start to slide the stilts;

3
Open your *Flip Book* to Lesson 12.
Enter each line twice.
Tap RETURN at the end of each line.
Don't correct mistakes.
When you finish, type each line in Bonus Lesson 12 twice.
You may begin.

Monitor the class for correct keyboarding position:
- ☑ *Wrists flat, elbows in, eyes on copy.*
- ☑ *Correct reach, anchoring, and return* HOME.
- ☑ *Steady rhythm, correct use of* SPACEBAR *and* RETURN.

End of Lesson 12

Lesson 13

Review

Materials

Student Flip Book

Key Review

| 1 | Check your keyboarding position. |

Pause and check.

| 2 | Clear ... seat ... feet ... fingers. |

| 3 | Let's review.
Get ready. |

| 4 |

iii ... HOME	ttt ... HOME	ooo ... HOME	rrr ... HOME
iii ... HOME	ooo ... HOME	rrr ... HOME	ttt ... HOME
kik kik	ftf ftf	lol lol	frf frf
itt ... HOME	itt ... HOME	or ... HOME	or ... HOME
ijk ijk	tal tal	rtr ... HOME	rtr ... HOME

Practice

1
Listen: if it sits;
You will enter words as I spell them.
Get ready.

Say and spell each word in Step 2.
Pause and say "SPACE" when appropriate.
Say "RETURN" at the end of the line.
Adjust dictation rate to the students' skill level.

2
if it sits; this state; lots of fir trees;
their last letter; at the third hit;
tried the third trail; ride the first jet;

3
Open your *Flip Book* to Lesson 13.
Enter each line twice.
Tap RETURN at the end of each line.
Don't correct mistakes.
When you finish, type each line in Bonus Lesson 13 twice.
You may begin.

Monitor the class for correct keyboarding position:
☑ *Wrists flat, elbows in, eyes on copy.*
☑ *Correct reach, anchoring, and return HOME.*
☑ *Steady rhythm, correct use of SPACEBAR and RETURN.*

End of Lesson 13

Lesson 14

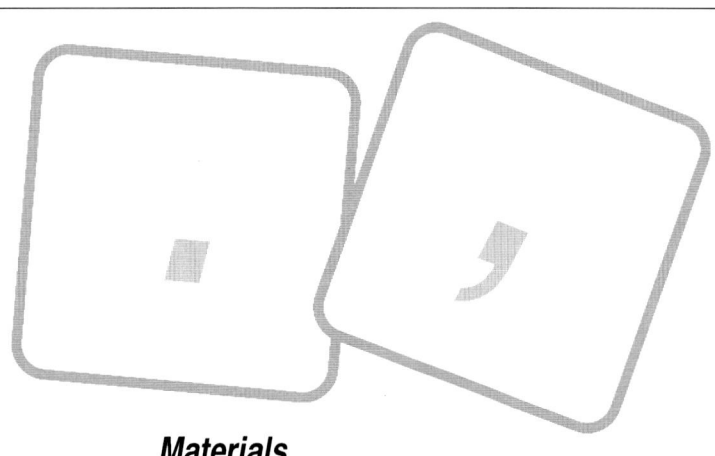

Keys Introduced

PERIOD   COMMA

Materials

Keyboard Wall Chart
Student Flip Book

Key Review

1 | Check your keyboarding position.

Pause and check.

2 | Clear ... seat ... feet ... fingers.

3 | Let's review. Get ready.

4 |
iii ... HOME	ttt ... HOME	ooo ... HOME	rrr ... HOME
ttt ... HOME	iii ... HOME	rrr ... HOME	ooo ... HOME
kik kik	ftf ftf	lol lol	frf frf
iki ... HOME	iki ... HOME	ftf oll	frr ... HOME
ftt ... HOME	loo ... HOME	rff rff	ftt ... HOME

Keyboard Success Teacher's Guide

Key Introduction: PERIOD COMMA

| 1 | Check your keyboarding position.

Pause and check.

| 2 | Clear ... seat ... feet ... fingers.

| 3 | You're going to learn two new keys.
Here's the PERIOD on the keyboard.

Touch the key on the Wall Chart.

| 4 | Use your right-hand ring finger.
Watch me reach down, tap PERIOD, and return HOME.

| 5 | Get ready.

Instruct students in a rhythmic manner.

| 6 | Tap PERIOD ... HOME ... PERIOD ... HOME ... PERIOD ... HOME.

| 7 | Let's practice with SPACES. Always tap the SPACEBAR once after a PERIOD or COMMA.
PERIOD ... HOME ... SPACE   PERIOD ... HOME ... SPACE
PERIOD ... HOME ... SPACE   l PERIOD l   l PERIOD l
l PERIOD l   l PERIOD l   l PERIOD l   l PERIOD l

70

Lesson 14 • PERIOD COMMA

8 | Now let's learn the COMMA.

Touch the key on the Wall Chart.

9 | Use your right-hand middle finger.
Watch me reach down, tap COMMA, and return HOME.
Always tap the SPACEBAR once after you tap COMMA.

10 | Get ready.

Instruct students in a rhythmic manner.

11 | Tap COMMA ... HOME ... SPACE   COMMA ... HOME ... SPACE
COMMA ... HOME ... SPACE.

12 | Let's practice with SPACES.
COMMA ... HOME ... SPACE   COMMA ... HOME ... SPACE
COMMA ... HOME ... SPACE   k COMMA k   k COMMA k
k COMMA k   k COMMA k   k COMMA k   k COMMA k

13 | Let's practice with both keys.
Get ready.

14 | PERIOD ... HOME ... SPACE   PERIOD ... HOME ... SPACE
l PERIOD l   l PERIOD l   l PERIOD l   l PERIOD l
COMMA ... HOME ... SPACE   COMMA ... HOME ... SPACE
COMMA ... HOME ... SPACE   k COMMA k   k COMMA k
k COMMA k   k COMMA k   k COMMA k   ll PERIOD ... HOME
lo PERIOD ... HOME   ki PERIOD ... HOME   ik COMMA ... HOME

Keyboard Success Teacher's Guide

Practice

1 Listen: the hot jail
You will enter words or letters as I spell them.
Get ready.

Say and spell each word or letter in Step 2.
Pause and say "SPACE" when appropriate.
Say "RETURN" at the end of the line.
Adjust dictation rate to the students' skill level.

2 the hot jail. the other three. if he does.
a, s, d, f, j, k, l. a, s, d, f, j, k, l. letters
had a flat tire. tore his toe, lie still.

3 Open your *Flip Book* to Lesson 14.
Enter each line twice.
Tap RETURN at the end of each line.
Don't correct mistakes.
When you finish, type each line in Bonus Lesson 14 twice.
You may begin.

Monitor the class for correct keyboarding position:
☑ *Wrists flat, elbows in, eyes on copy.*
☑ *Correct reach, anchoring, and return* HOME.
☑ *Steady rhythm, correct use of* SPACEBAR *and* RETURN.

End of Lesson 14

Lesson 15

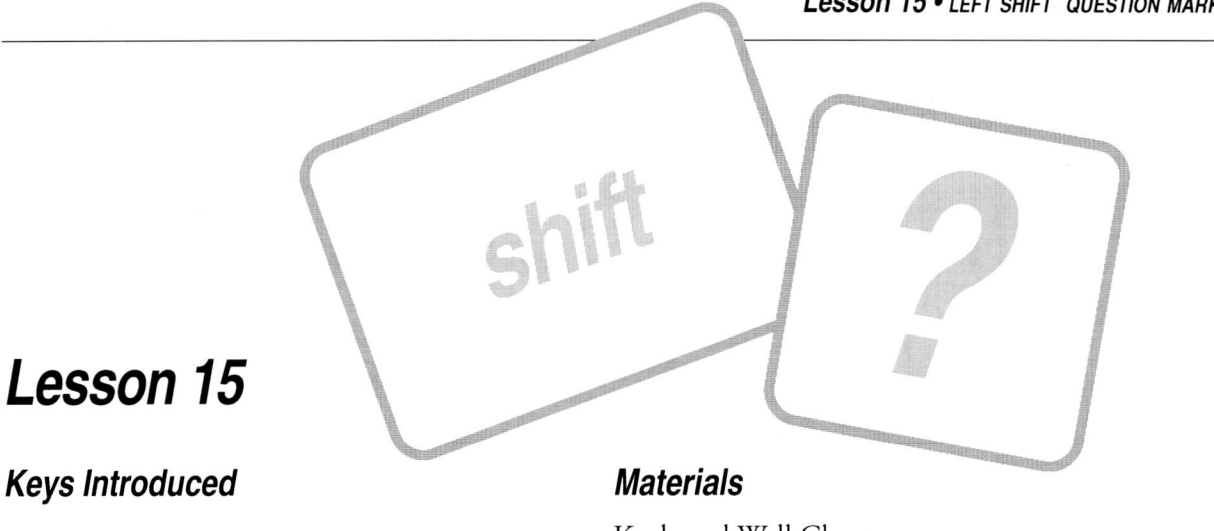

Keys Introduced

LEFT SHIFT   QUESTION MARK

Materials

Keyboard Wall Chart
Student Flip Book

Key Review

1 | Check your keyboarding position.

Pause and check.

2 | Clear ... seat ... feet ... fingers.

3 | Let's review.
Get ready.

4 |
PERIOD PERIOD PERIOD ... HOME   ,,, ... HOME   ,,, ... HOME
PERIOD PERIOD PERIOD ... HOME   ,,, ... HOME   iii ... HOME
,,, ... HOME   ttt ... HOME   PERIOD PERIOD PERIOD ... HOME
k,k   kik   l.l   ftf   k,k   l.d   ll PERIOD ... HOME
kik   ftf   ftf   k,k   ll, ... HOME   kk, ... HOME
ll PERIOD ... HOME   kl PERIOD ... HOME   lk, ... HOME
kl, ... HOME   lk PERIOD ... HOME   l PERIOD , ... HOME

Keyboard Success Teacher's Guide

Key Introduction: LEFT SHIFT QUESTION MARK

1 | Check your keyboarding position.

Pause and check.

2 | Clear ... seat ... feet ... fingers.

3 | You're going to learn how to enter capital and lowercase letters.

Touch the LEFT SHIFT key on the Wall Chart.

4 | This is the LEFT SHIFT key.
The LEFT SHIFT key lets you capitalize letters or use two-character keys.

5 | Use your left-hand little finger to hold the LEFT SHIFT key down.
Watch me reach over, hold down LEFT SHIFT, and tap K.
Watch me release the LEFT SHIFT key and return HOME.

6 | Get ready to capitalize.
Reach down with your left-hand little finger and hold LEFT SHIFT down.

Pause.

7 | Keep LEFT SHIFT down and tap capital K.

Pause.

Lesson 15 • LEFT SHIFT QUESTION MARK

8   Release LEFT SHIFT and return HOME.

9   Let's capitalize another letter.
Reach down with your left-hand little finger and hold LEFT SHIFT down.

Pause.

10   Keep LEFT SHIFT down and tap capital J.

Pause.

11   Release LEFT SHIFT and return HOME.

12   Enter the letters I say.
Only capitalize letters when I say LEFT SHIFT.
    j   LEFT SHIFT O … HOME   LEFT SHIFT J

13   Now let's learn the QUESTION MARK.

Touch the key on the Wall Chart.

14   Press LEFT SHIFT and hold it down.
Use your right-hand little finger.
Watch me reach down, hold down LEFT SHIFT, tap QUESTION MARK, and return HOME.
At the end of a sentence always tap the SPACEBAR one time after a PERIOD or a QUESTION MARK.

| 15 | Get ready.

Instruct students in a rhythmic manner.

| 16 | Tap LEFT SHIFT ... QUESTION MARK ... HOME ... SPACE
LEFT SHIFT ... QUESTION MARK ... HOME ... SPACE
LEFT SHIFT ... QUESTION MARK ... HOME ... SPACE
l; ... LEFT SHIFT ... QUESTION MARK ... HOME
k; ... LEFT SHIFT ... QUESTION MARK ... HOME

| 17 | Let's practice LEFT SHIFT and QUESTION MARK.
Get ready.

| 18 | LEFT SHIFT ... QUESTION MARK ... HOME ... SPACE
LEFT SHIFT ... QUESTION MARK ... HOME ... SPACE
LEFT SHIFT ... l ... QUESTION MARK ... HOME ... SPACE
LEFT SHIFT ... QUESTION MARK ... QUESTION MARK ... HOME ... SPACE
l ... LEFT SHIFT ... QUESTION MARK ... HOME

Lesson 15 • LEFT SHIFT QUESTION MARK

Practice

1 | Listen: Oskar ate his toast.
You will enter words as I spell them.
Get ready.

Say and spell each word in Step 2.
Pause and say "SPACE" when appropriate.
Say "RETURN" at the end of the line.
Adjust dictation rate to the students' skill level.

2 | Oskar ate his toast. Is Kerri tired?
Is that a toad? I still see Oak Lake.
Had Lisa, Kae, or Joel lost? Is it his?

3 | Open your *Flip Book* to Lesson 15.
Enter each line twice.
Tap RETURN at the end of each line.
Don't correct mistakes.
When you finish, type the text in Bonus Lesson 15 twice.
You may begin.

Monitor the class for correct keyboarding technique:
☑ *Wrists flat, elbows in, eyes on copy.*
☑ *Correct reach, anchoring, and return HOME.*
☑ *Steady rhythm, correct use of SPACEBAR and RETURN.*

End of Lesson 15

Lesson 16 • Review and Timed Practice

Lesson 16

Review and Timed Practice

Materials

Watch/clock with a second hand
Student Flip Book

Key Review

1 | Check your keyboarding position.

Pause and check.

2 | Clear ... seat ... feet ... fingers.

3 | Let's review.
Get ready.

4 |
iii ... HOME	ttt ... HOME	,,, ... HOME	??? ... HOM
ftf ftf	tft ... HOME	;?; ;?;	kik kik
l.l l.l	k,k k,k	ki, ... HOME	ki, ... HOME
tff tff	ftt ... HOME	;?; ;?;	;?; ;?;

5 | Let's review LEFT SHIFT.

6 LEFT SHIFT H? ... HOME ... SPACE
LEFT SHIFT I? ... HOME ... SPACE
LEFT SHIFT H? ... HOME ... SPACE
LEFT SHIFT I? ... HOME ... SPACE

Practice

1 Listen: Is Jed late for his date, Karla Oakes?
You will enter words as I spell them.
Get ready.

Say and spell each word in Step 2.
Pause and say "SPACE" when appropriate.
Say "RETURN" at the end of the line.
Adjust dictation rate to the students' skill level.

2 Is Jed late for his date, Karla Oakes?
Look after Kelli Kale. Ollie Hill hides.
O.K., Lissa, or Jake hate hot fried eel.

3 Open your *Flip Book* to Lesson 16.
Enter each line twice.
Tap RETURN at the end of each line.
Don't correct mistakes.
When you finish, enter each line in Bonus Lesson 16 twice.
You may begin.

Monitor the class for correct keyboarding technique:
☑ Wrists flat, elbows in, eyes on copy.
☑ Correct reach, anchoring, and return HOME.
☑ Steady rhythm, correct use of SPACEBAR and RETURN.

Lesson 16 • Review and Timed Practice

Keyboarding Rate

- *This lesson includes timed practice for keys introduced in Lessons 2–10. To accurately measure students' progress in the program, it is important to obtain this data.*

- *You will need a watch or a clock with a second hand.*

- *Important Note: The following script assumes that students will save their timed practice drills to a disk for you to check on screen or in printed form after the lesson. If the equipment students are using will not save files or if you prefer to collect this information in another manner, you will need to adjust the following instructions.*

| 1 | You're going to practice keyboarding as quickly and accurately as you can for 1 minute. You won't be graded; but I will compare your keyboarding speed in this exercise with your rate in the last timed exercise, so type quickly but carefully. |

| 2 | Look at Bonus Lesson 16 again. |

Check.

| 3 | Touch the group of three lines. |

Check.

Keyboard Success Teacher's Guide

4 | When I say begin, type the three lines one after the other as many times as you can.
Tap RETURN at the end of each line.
Try not to look at your fingers.
Don't correct mistakes.
I will stop you after 1 minute.

5 | Check your keyboarding position.

Pause.

6 | Ready ... begin.

Allow 1 minute.

7 | Stop.

Have students save their timed keyboarding work to a disk to hand in.

8 | Now save your work to your disk and leave the disk with me.

After the lesson, review the students' work, either on screen or in printed form, for speed and accuracy.

Calculating Gross Words A Minute (GWAM)

1 Count the total number of full lines typed during the 1-minute interval and place on Line A.

Multiply the number of lines by 6 to obtain a preliminary word count. (Each line contains the equivalent of 6 words or 30 characters.) Place on Line B.

2 Count the number of letters, punctuation marks, and spaces in a partially typed line. Place on Line C.

Divide the number of characters by 5 to calculate the number of words in the partially typed line. Place on Line D.

3 Add Lines B & D to obtain student's GWAM.

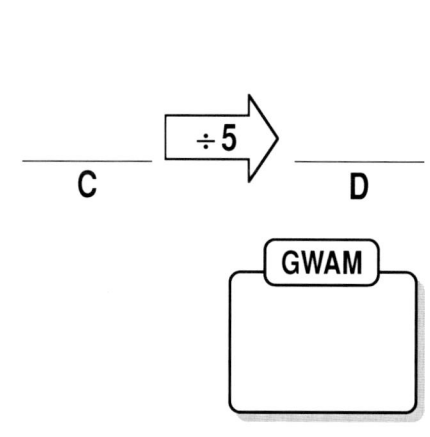

Record this number in the first column for Lesson 16 on the Record Grid for Handwriting and Keyboarding Rates.

In the second column ot the Record Grid, record the total number of words typed without error.

You may wish to provide students with a written report for each timed practice. A template for this purpose is provided in the Appendix. Copy and complete one form for each student.

End of Lesson 16

Lesson 17 • u c

Lesson 17

Keys Introduced

u   c

Materials

Keyboard Wall Chart
Student Flip Book

Key Review

1 | Check your keyboarding position.

Pause and check.

2 | Clear ... seat ... feet ... fingers.

3 | Let's review.
Get ready.

4 |
ttt ... HOME	l.l l.l	,,, ... HOME	iii ... HOME
??? ... HOME	iii ... HOME	ttt ... HOME	iii ... HOME
??? ... HOME	l.l l.l	.lo ... HOME	.lo ... HOME
ftf ftt	kik kik	kik ikk	ki, ... HOME
ki, ... HOME	lol ftf	;?; lol	ftf ;?;

85

Keyboard Success Teacher's Guide

Key Introduction: u c

| 1 | Check your keyboarding position.

Pause and check.

| 2 | Clear ... seat ... feet ... fingers.

| 3 | You're going to learn two new keys.
Here's u on the keyboard.

Touch the key on the Wall Chart.

| 4 | Use your right-hand pointer finger.
Watch me reach up, tap u, and return HOME.

| 5 | Get ready.

Instruct students in a rhythmic manner.

| 6 | Tap u ... HOME ... u ... HOME ... u ... HOME.

| 7 | Let's practice with SPACES.
uuu ... HOME   uuu ... HOME   uuu ... HOME   uuu ... HOME
uuu ... HOME   juj   juj   juj   juj   juj   juj
juj   juj   juj   juj   uuu ... HOME   uuu ... HOME

Lesson 17 • u c

8 Now let's learn c.

Touch the key on the Wall Chart.

9 Use your left-hand middle finger.
Watch me reach down, tap c, and return HOME.
When you reach for a key, keep your other fingers anchored.

10 Get ready.

Instruct students in a rhythmic manner.

11 Tap c ... HOME ... c ... HOME ... c ... HOME.

12 Let's practice with SPACES.

ccc ... HOME	ccc ... HOME	ccc ... HOME	ccc ... HOME
ccc ... HOME	dcd dcd	dcd dcd	dcd dcd
dcd dcd	dcd dcd	ccc ... HOME	ccc ... HOME

13 Let's practice with both keys.
Get ready.

14

uuu ... HOME	uuu ... HOME	uuu ... HOME	uuu ... HOME
uuu ... HOME	juj juj	juj juj	juj juj
juj juj	juj juj	ccc ... HOME	ccc ... HOME
ccc ... HOME	ccc ... HOME	ccc ... HOME	dcd dcd
dcd dcd	dcd dcd	dcd dcd	dec ... HOME
ced dec ... HOME	juj juu ... HOME	ced dec ... HOME

Keyboard Success Teacher's Guide

Practice

1 Listen: Kris sees crackers at the couch.
You will enter words as I spell them.
Get ready.

Say and spell each word in Step 2.
Pause and say "SPACE" when appropriate.
Say "RETURN" at the end of the line.
Adjust dictation rate to the students' skill level.

2 Kris sees crackers at the couch.
Judd uses flour to create four tart crusts.
Hurrah, our soccer star scored. Hurrah.

3 Open your *Flip Book* to Lesson 17.
Enter each line twice.
Tap RETURN at the end of each line.
Don't correct mistakes.
When you finish, enter the text in Bonus Lesson 17 twice.
You may begin.

Monitor the class for correct keyboarding technique:
☑ *Wrists flat, elbows in, eyes on copy.*
☑ *Correct reach, anchoring, and return HOME.*
☑ *Steady rhythm, correct use of SPACEBAR and RETURN.*

End of Lesson 15

Lesson 18

Review

Materials

Student Flip Book

Key Review

1 | Check your keyboarding position.

Pause and check.

2 | Clear ... seat ... feet ... fingers.

3 | Let's review.
Get ready.

4

uuu ... HOME	ccc ... HOME	??? ... HOME	ccc ... HOME
uuu ... HOME	??? ... HOME	uuu ... HOME	ccc ... HOME
juj dcd	?;? ... HOME	dcd juj	?;? ... HOME
juj dcd	cu? ... HOME	ju? ... HOME	du? ... HOME

Practice

1 | Listen: I hear our ukulele call.
You will enter words as I spell them.
Get ready.

Say and spell each word in Step 2.
Pause and say "SPACE" when appropriate.
Say "RETURN" at the end of the line.
Adjust dictation rate to the students' skill level.

2 | I hear our ukulele call. I trust Lulu.
Is the circus here? Ice Lake is so cold.
Jack tells such useless facts. It is ice.

3 | Open your *Flip Book* to Lesson 18.
Enter each line twice.
Tap RETURN at the end of each line.
Don't correct mistakes.
When you finish, enter the text in Bonus Lesson 18 twice.
You may begin.

Monitor the class for correct keyboarding technique:
☑ *Wrists flat, elbows in, eyes on copy.*
☑ *Correct reach, anchoring, and return* HOME.
☑ *Steady rhythm, correct use of* SPACEBAR *and* RETURN.

End of Lesson 18

Lesson 19 • n w

Lesson 19

Keys Introduced

n w

Materials

Keyboard Wall Chart
Student Flip Book

Key Review

1 | Check your keyboarding position.

Pause and check.

2 | Clear ... seat ... feet ... fingers.

3 | Let's review.
Get ready.

4 | ccc ... HOME   uuu ... HOME   ccc ... HOME   uuu ... HOME
??? ... HOME   ccc ... HOME   ??? ... HOME   uuu ... HOME
ccc ... HOME   dcd   juj   ?;? ... HOME   juj   dcd
??? ... HOME   juj   dcd   juj   dcd   du? ... HOME
jc;   cu? ... HOME   ju;   dc? ... HOME   cj;   uc? ... HOME

91

Key Introduction: n w

1 Check your keyboarding position.

Pause and check.

2 Clear ... seat ... feet ... fingers.

3 You're going to learn two new keys. Here's n on the keyboard.

Touch the key on the Wall Chart.

4 Use your right-hand pointer finger.
Watch me reach down, tap n, and return HOME.
When you reach for a key, keep your other fingers anchored.

5 Get ready.

Instruct students in a rhythmic manner.

6 Tap n ... HOME ... n ... HOME ... n ... HOME.

7 Let's practice with spaces.

8
nnn ... HOME   nnn ... HOME   nnn ... HOME   nnn ... HOME
nnn ... HOME   nnn ... HOME   jnj   jnj   jnj   jnj
jnj   jnj   jnj   jnj   jnj   jnj   jnj   jnj

Lesson 19 • n w

9 Now let's learn w.

Touch the key on the Wall Chart.

10 Use your left-hand ring finger.
Watch me reach up, tap w, and return HOME.

11 Get ready.

Instruct students in a rhythmic manner.

12 Tap w ... HOME ... w ... HOME ... w ... HOME.

13 Let's practice with spaces.

www ... HOME	www ... HOME	www ... HOME	www ... HOME
www ... HOME	www ... HOME	sws	sws	sws	sws
sws	sws	sws	sws	sws	sws	sws	sws

14 Let's practice with both keys.
Get ready.

15

nnn ... HOME	nnn ... HOME	nnn ... HOME	nnn ... HOME
nnn ... HOME	jnj	jnj	jnj	jnj	jnj	jnj
jnj	jnj	jnj	jnj	www ... HOME	www ... HOME
www ... HOME	www ... HOME	www ... HOME	sws	sws
sws	sws	sws	sws	sws	sws	sws	wss
wsw ... HOME	jun ... HOME	jhn ... HOME	jun ... HOME

Practice

1 Listen: Nonie cannot land one.
You will enter words as I spell them.
Get ready.

Say and spell each word in Step 2.
Pause and say "SPACE" when appropriate.
Say "RETURN" at the end of the line.
Adjust dictation rate to the students' skill level.

2 Nonie cannot land one. Ned wants Nikes.
He will know the weather. How did I win?
Our cow chewed her cud. Nan is a friend.

3 Open your *Flip Book* to Lesson 19.
Enter each line twice.
Tap RETURN at the end of each line.
Don't correct mistakes.
When you finish, enter the text in Bonus Lesson 19 twice.
You may begin.

Monitor the class for correct keyboarding technique:
☑ *Wrists flat, elbows in, eyes on copy.*
☑ *Correct reach, anchoring, and return HOME.*
☑ *Steady rhythm, correct use of SPACEBAR and RETURN.*

End of Lesson 19

Lesson 20 • g RIGHT SHIFT EXCLAMATION POINT

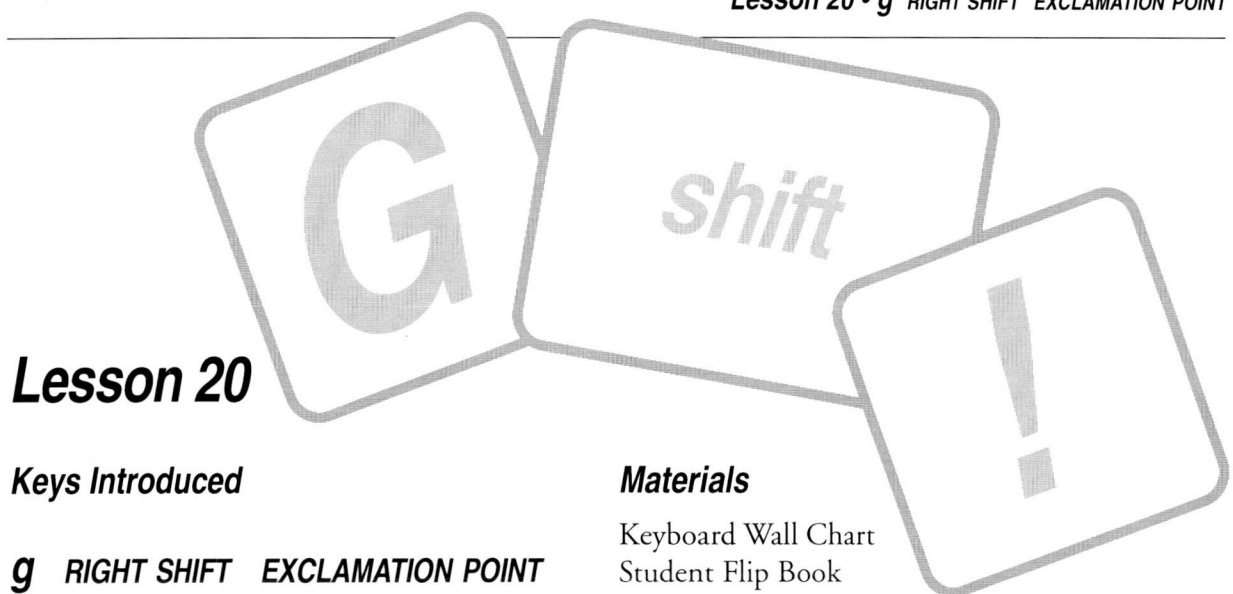

Lesson 20

Keys Introduced

g RIGHT SHIFT EXCLAMATION POINT

Materials

Keyboard Wall Chart
Student Flip Book

Key Review

| 1 | Check your keyboarding position. |

Pause and check.

| 2 | Clear ... seat ... feet ... fingers. |

| 3 | Let's review.
Get ready. |

| 4 | uuu ... HOME   ccc ... HOME   nnn ... HOME   www ... HOME
uuu ... HOME   www ... HOME   ccc ... HOME   nnn ... HOME
jnj   jnj;   dcd   dcd;   juj   juj   sws   sws
jun ... HOME   jun, ... HOME   dec ... HOME   dec, ... HOME |

95

Keyboard Success Teacher's Guide

Key Introduction: g RIGHT SHIFT EXCLAMATION POINT

1 | Check your keyboarding position.

Pause and check.

2 | Clear ... seat ... feet ... fingers.

3 | You're going to learn two new keys.
Here's g on the keyboard.

Touch the key on the Wall Chart.

4 | Use your left-hand pointer finger.
Watch me reach over, tap g, and return HOME.

5 | Get ready.

Instruct students in a rhythmic manner.

6 | Tap g ... HOME ... g ... HOME ... g ... HOME.

7 | Let's practice with SPACES.
ggg ... HOME	ggg ... HOME	ggg ... HOME	ggg ... HOME
ggg ... HOME	ggg ... HOME	fgf fgf	fgf fgf
fgf fgf	fgf fgf	fgf fgf	fgf fgf

Lesson 20 • g RIGHT SHIFT EXCLAMATION POINT

8 You're going to learn how to use the RIGHT SHIFT key.

Touch the RIGHT SHIFT key on the Wall Chart.

9 This key is called RIGHT SHIFT.
RIGHT SHIFT lets you capitalize letters or use two-character keys.
Use your right-hand little finger and hold RIGHT SHIFT down.
Watch me hold down the RIGHT SHIFT and tap D.

10 Get ready.
Reach down with your right-hand little finger and hold RIGHT SHIFT down.

Pause and check.

11 Keep RIGHT SHIFT down and tap capital D. Release the RIGHT SHIFT key.
Hold RIGHT SHIFT down and tap capital R ... HOME. Release RIGHT SHIFT.

12 Enter the letters that I say.

Pause after each letter.

13 RIGHT SHIFT with your right hand, tap capital C ... HOME.
Lowercase f
RIGHT SHIFT with your right hand, tap capital A.
Lowercase w ... HOME.

Repeat the procedure in Step 13 without prompting students to RIGHT SHIFT.

Keyboard Success Teacher's Guide

Touch the EXCLAMATION POINT *key on the Wall Chart.*

14 Some keys have two characters on them. On your keyboard, this key has the number 1 and an EXCLAMATION POINT.

15 The LEFT SHIFT or RIGHT SHIFT key lets you enter the top character on any two-character key.

16 Enter the character I say.
RIGHT SHIFT with your right hand, tap EXCLAMATION POINT.
Release RIGHT SHIFT, tap the number 1.

Repeat the procedure in Step 16 without prompting students to RIGHT SHIFT.

Practice

1 Listen: Gigi gags the goose.
You will enter words as I spell them.
Get ready.

Say and spell each word in Step 2.
*Pause and say "*SPACE*" when appropriate.*
*Say "*RETURN*" at the end of the line.*
Adjust dictation rate to the students' skill level.

2 Gigi gags the goose. The goslings go!
When will Elsa grin? Gina is digging.
Tigger is a tiger. Greta wears goggles!

Lesson 20 • g *RIGHT SHIFT EXCLAMATION POINT*

3 | Open your *Flip Book* to Lesson 20.
Enter each line twice.
Tap RETURN at the end of each line.
Don't correct mistakes.
When you finish, enter the text in Bonus Lesson 20 twice.
You may begin.

Monitor the class for correct keyboarding technique:
☑ *Wrists flat, elbows in, eyes on copy.*
☑ *Correct reach, anchoring, and return HOME.*
☑ *Steady rhythm, correct use of SPACEBAR and RETURN.*

End of Lesson 20

Lesson 21

Review

Materials

Student Flip Book

Key Review

1 Check your keyboarding position.

Pause and check.

2 Clear ... seat ... feet ... fingers.

3 Let's review. Get ready.

4
ggg ... HOME	www ... HOME	ccc ... HOME	nnn ... HOME
ggg ... HOME	nnn ... HOME	www ... HOME	fgf fgf
jnj jnj	sws sws	fgt ... HOME	fgt ... HOME
jnh ... HOME	jnh ... HOME	sws swa	sws swa

5 Let's review SHIFT.
RIGHT SHIFT S
RIGHT SHIFT W ... HOME
RIGHT SHIFT RFD

Practice

1
Listen: Roger is not going.
You will enter words as I spell them.
Get ready.

Say and spell each word in Step 2.
Pause and say "SPACE" when appropriate.
Say "RETURN" at the end of the line.
Adjust dictation rate to the students' skill level.

2
Roger is not going. Ted gets to go now!
Where is Sarah? She giggles with Gina.
Don gets a goat. Sue juggles oranges.

3
Open your *Flip Book* to Lesson 21.
Enter each line twice.
Tap RETURN at the end of each line.
Don't correct mistakes.
When you finish, enter the text in Bonus Lesson 21 twice.
You may begin.

Monitor the class for correct keyboarding technique:
- ☑ *Clear ... seat ... feet ... fingers.*
- ☑ *Correct reach, anchoring, and return HOME.*
- ☑ *Use correct finger for each SHIFT key.*

End of Lesson 21

Lesson 22 • m b

Lesson 22

Keys Introduced

m   b

Materials

Keyboard Wall Chart
Student Flip Book

Key Review

| 1 | Check your keyboarding position.

Pause and check.

| 2 | Clear ... seat ... feet ... fingers.

| 3 | Let's review.
Get ready.

| 4 |
ggg ... HOME	nnn ... HOME	www ... HOME	ggg ... HOME
nnn ... HOME	www ... HOME	ggg ... HOME	www ... HOME
fgf jnj	sws fgf	jnj sws	fgf sws
fgt ... HOME	jnu ... HOME	jun ... HOME	fgf swa

Keyboard Success Teacher's Guide

Key Introduction: m b

| 1 | Check your keyboarding position. |

Pause and check.

| 2 | Clear … seat … feet … fingers. |

| 3 | You're going to learn two new keys.
Here's m on the keyboard. |

Touch the key on the Wall Chart.

| 4 | Use your right-hand pointer finger.
Watch me reach down, tap m, and return HOME. |

| 5 | Get ready. |

Instruct students in a rhythmic manner.

| 6 | Tap m … HOME … m … HOME … m … HOME. |

| 7 | Let's practice with SPACES.
mmm … HOME   mmm … HOME   mmm … HOME   mmm … HOME
mmm … HOME   mmm … HOME   jmj   jmj   jmj   jmj
jmj   jmj   jmj   jmj   jmj   jmj   jmj   jmj |

Lesson 22 • m b

8 | Now let's learn b.

Touch the key on the Wall Chart.

9 | Use your left-hand pointer finger.
Watch me reach down and over, tap b, and return HOME.

10 | Get ready.

Instruct students in a rhythmic manner.

11 | Tap b ... HOME ... b ... HOME ... b ... HOME.

12 | Let's practice with SPACES.
bbb ... HOME   bbb ... HOME   bbb ... HOME   bbb ... HOME
bbb ... HOME   bbb ... HOME   fbf   fbf   fbf   fbf
fbf   fbf   fbf   fbf   fbf   fbf   fbf   fbf

13 | Let's practice with both keys.
Get ready.

14 | mmm ... HOME   mmm ... HOME   mmm ... HOME   mmm ... HOME
jmj   jmj   jmj   jmj   jmj   jmj   jmj   jmj
bbb ... HOME   bbb ... HOME   bbb ... HOME   bbb ... HOME
fbf   fbf   fbf   fbf   fbf   fbf   fbf   fbf
mmj   jmj   mmj   jmj   mmj   jmj   mmj   jmj
fgb ... HOME   tfb ... HOME   fbg ... HOME   tfb ... HOME

Keyboard Success Teacher's Guide

Practice

1 Listen: Mama melted marshmallows.
You will enter words as I spell them.
Get ready.

Say and spell each word in Step 2.
Pause and say "SPACE" when appropriate.
Say "RETURN" at the end of the line.
Adjust dictation rate to the students' skill level.

2 Mama melted marshmallows. Make nine!
Bob Budd hobbled to the scrabble board.
Mom found brontosaurus fossils in Maine.

3 Open your *Flip Book* to Lesson 22.
Enter each line twice.
Tap RETURN at the end of each line.
Don't correct mistakes.
When you finish, enter the text in Bonus Lesson 22 twice.
You may begin.

Monitor the class for correct keyboarding technique:
☑ *Clear ... seat ... feet ... fingers.*
☑ *Correct reach, anchoring, and return HOME.*
☑ *Using correct fingers for each SHIFT.*

End of Lesson 22

Lesson 23

Review and Timed Practice

Materials

Watch/clock with a second hand
Student Flip Book

Key Review

1 | Check your keyboarding position.

Pause and check.

2 | Clear ... seat ... feet ... fingers.

3 | Let's review.
Get ready.

4

mmm ... HOME	bbb ... HOME	ggg ... HOME	mmm ... HOME
bbb ... HOME	ggg ... HOME	mmm ... HOME	ggg ... HOME
bbb ... HOME	mmm ... HOME	jmj fbf	fgf jmj
fbf fgf	jmj fgf	jmj fbf	jhm ... HOME
fgb ... HOME	ftb ... HOME	jum ... HOME	fgb ... HOME
ftb ... HOME	fmh ... HOME	ftb ... HOME	jhm ... HOME

Practice

1 Listen: Mama and Marie made a major mistake!
You will enter words as I spell them.
Get ready.

*Say and spell each word in Step 2.
Pause and say "SPACE" when appropriate.
Say "RETURN" at the end of the line.
Adjust dictation rate to the students' skill level.*

2 Mama and Marie made a major mistake!
Babies babble; black bumble bees bite.
Am I unable to remember his best fables?

3 Open your *Flip Book* to Lesson 23.
Enter each line twice.
Tap RETURN at the end of each line.
Don't correct mistakes.
When you finish, enter each line in Bonus Lesson 23 twice.
You may begin.

Monitor the class for correct keyboarding technique:
☑ *Clear ... seat ... feet ... fingers.*
☑ *Correct reach, anchoring, and return HOME.*
☑ *Using correct fingers for each SHIFT.*

Lesson 23 • Review and Timed Practice

Keyboarding Rate

- *This lesson includes timed practice for keys introduced in Lessons 2–17. To accurately measure students' progress in the program, it is important to obtain this data.*

- *You will need a watch or a clock with a second hand.*

- *Important Note: The following script assumes that students will save their timed practice drills to a disk for you to check on screen or in printed form after the lesson. If the equipment students are using will not save files or if you prefer to collect this information in another manner, you will need to adjust the following instructions.*

1 | You're going to practice keyboarding as quickly and accurately as you can for 1 minute. You won't be graded; but I will compare your keyboarding speed in this exercise with your rate in the last timed exercise, so type quickly but carefully.

2 | Look at Bonus Lesson 23 again.

Check.

3 | Touch the group of three lines.

Check.

4 | When I say begin, type the three lines one after the other as many times as you can.
Tap RETURN at the end of each line.
Try not to look at your fingers.
Don't correct mistakes.
I will stop you after 1 minute.

5 | Check your keyboarding position.

Pause.

6 | Ready ... begin.

Allow 1 minute.

7 | Stop.

Have students save their timed keyboarding work to a disk to hand in.

8 | Now save your work to your disk and leave the disk with me.

After the lesson, review the students' work, either on screen or in printed form, for speed and accuracy.

Lesson 23 • Review and Timed Practice

Calculating Gross Words A Minute (GWAM)

1 Count the total number of full lines typed during the 1-minute interval and place on Line A.

Multiply the number of lines by 6 to obtain a preliminary word count. (Each line contains the equivalent of 6 words or 30 characters.) Place on Line B.

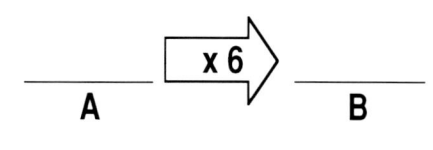

2 Count the number of letters, punctuation marks, and spaces in a partially typed line. Place on Line C.

Divide the number of characters by 5 to calculate the number of words in the partially typed line. Place on Line D.

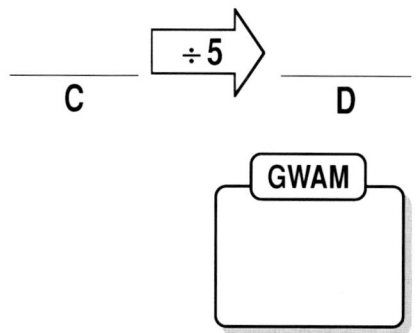

3 Add Lines B & D to obtain student's GWAM.

Record this number in the first column for Lesson 23 on the Record Grid for Handwriting and Keyboarding Rates.

In the second column of the Record Grid, record the total number of words typed without error.

You may wish to provide students with a written report for each timed practice. A template for this purpose is provided in the Appendix. Copy and complete one form for each student.

End of Lesson 23

Lesson 24

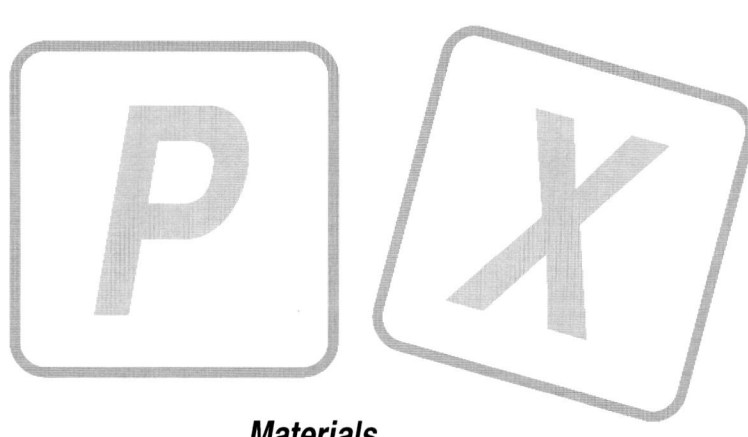

Keys Introduced

p   x

Materials

Keyboard Wall Chart
Student Flip Book

Key Review

1 | Check your keyboarding position.

Pause and check.

2 | Clear ... seat ... feet ... fingers.

3 | Let's review.
Get ready.

4 |
ggg ... HOME	mmm ... HOME	bbb ... HOME	nnn ... HOME
www ... HOME	bbb ... HOME	ggg ... HOME	mmm ... HOME
fgf fgf;	jmj jmj	fbf fbf;	jnj sws
jum ... HOME	jum ... HOME	fgt ... HOME	fbf, ... HOME
fbg ... HOME	bft ... HOME	fgt ... HOME	fbg ... HOME

Keyboard Success Teacher's Guide

Key Introduction: p x

| 1 | Check your keyboarding position. |

Pause and check.

| 2 | Clear ... seat ... feet ... fingers. |

| 3 | You're going to learn two new keys.
Here's p on the keyboard. |

Touch the key on the Wall Chart.

| 4 | Use your right-hand little finger.
Watch me reach up, tap p, and return HOME. |

| 5 | Get ready. |

Instruct students in a rhythmic manner.

| 6 | Tap p ... HOME ... p ... HOME ... p ... HOME. |

| 7 | Let's practice with SPACES.
ppp ... HOME   ppp ... HOME   ppp ... HOME   ppp ... HOME
ppp ... HOME   ppp ... HOME   ;p;   ;p;   ;p   ;p;
;p;   ;p;   ;p;   ;p;   ;p;   ;p;   ;p;   ;p; |

Lesson 24 • p x

8 | Now let's learn x.

Touch the key on the Wall Chart.

9 | Use your left-hand ring finger.
Watch me reach down, tap x, and return HOME.

10 | Get ready.

Instruct students in a rhythmic manner.

11 | Tap x … HOME … x … HOME … x … HOME.

12 | Let's practice with SPACES.
xxx … HOME	xxx … HOME	xxx … HOME	xxx … HOME
xxx … HOME	xxx … HOME	sxs sxs	sxs sxs
sxs sxs	sxs sxs	sxs sxs	sxs sxs

13 | Let's practice with both keys.
Get ready.

14 |
ppp … HOME	ppp … HOME	ppp … HOME	ppp … HOME
ppp … HOME	;p; ;p;	;p; ;p;	;p; ;p;
;p; ;p;	;p; ;p;	xxx … HOME	xxx … HOME
xxx … HOME	xxx … HOME	xxx … HOME	sxs sxs
sxs sxs	sxs sxs	sxs sxs	sxs sxs
wsx … HOME	wsx … HOME	sxw … HOME	p?p … HOME

Practice

1 Listen: Max and Tex mix sixteen boxes of jello.
You will enter words as I spell them.
Get ready.

Say and spell each word in Step 2.
Pause and say "SPACE" when appropriate.
Say "RETURN" at the end of the line.
Adjust dictation rate to the students' skill level.

2 Max and Tex mix sixteen boxes of jello.
Rex brought a purple puppet from Mexico.
Pearl, will Pam please pass the peas?

3 Open your *Flip Book* to Lesson 24.
Enter each line twice.
Tap RETURN at the end of each line.
Don't correct mistakes.
When you finish, enter the text in Bonus Lesson 24 twice.
You may begin.

Monitor the class for correct keyboarding technique:
☑ *Clear ... seat ... feet ... fingers.*
☑ *Correct reach, anchoring, and return HOME.*
☑ *Using correct fingers for each SHIFT.*

End of Lesson 24

Lesson 25

Review

Materials

Student Flip Book

Key Review

1 Check your keyboarding position.

Pause and check.

2 Clear ... seat ... feet ... fingers.

3 Let's review.
Get ready.

4
ppp ... HOME	xxx ... HOME	mmm ... HOME	bbb ... HOME
mmm ... HOME	xxx ... HOME	bbb ... HOME	ppp ... HOME
;p; ;p;	sxs sxs,	jmj jmj,	fbf fbf
fbg ... HOME	fgb ... HOME	swx ... HOME	swx ... HOME
;p; ;?;	;p? ... HOME	jum ... HOME	jum ... HOME

Keyboard Success Teacher's Guide

Practice

1 Listen: People plant peach, pear, and plum trees.
You will enter words as I spell them.
Get ready.

Say and spell each word in Step 2.
Pause and say "SPACE" when appropriate.
Say "RETURN" at the end of the line.
Adjust dictation rate to the students' skill level.

2 People plant peach, pear, and plum trees.
Max plans to relax in Mexico or Texas.
Will Patti take a maximum of six exams?

3 Open your *Flip Book* to Lesson 25.
Enter each line twice.
Tap RETURN at the end of each line.
Don't correct mistakes.
When you finish, enter the text in Bonus Lesson 25 twice.
You may begin.

Monitor the class for correct keyboarding technique:
☑ *Clear ... seat ... feet ... fingers.*
☑ *Correct reach, anchoring, and return HOME.*
☑ *Using correct fingers for each SHIFT.*

End of Lesson 25

Lesson 26 • y z

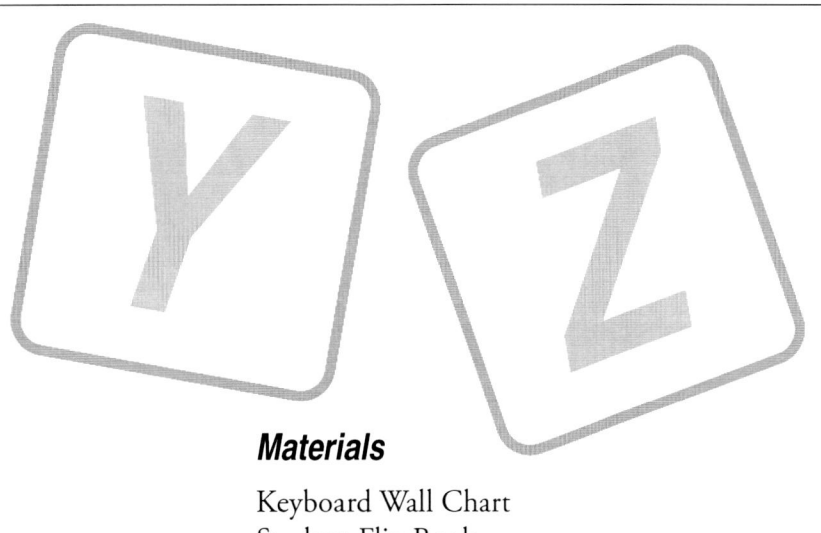

Lesson 26

Keys Introduced

y   z

Materials

Keyboard Wall Chart
Student Flip Book

Key Review

1 | Check your keyboarding position.

Pause and check.

2 | Clear ... seat ... feet ... fingers.

3 | Let's review.
Get ready.

4 |
ppp ... HOME	xxx ... HOME	mmm ... HOME	bbb ... HOME
ppp ... HOME	xxx ... HOME	mmm ... HOME	bbb ... HOME
p;p sxs	jmm ... HOME	fbf fbf	jmm ... HOME
sxs p;p	;p? ... HOME	swx ... HOME	jhm ... HOME
jum ... HOME	fgb ... HOME	;?p ... HOME	swx ... HOME
jhm ... HOME	fgb ... HOME	;?p ... HOME	swx ... HOME

Keyboard Success Teacher's Guide

Key Introduction: y z

| 1 | Check your keyboarding position. |

Pause and check.

| 2 | Clear ... seat ... feet ... fingers. |

| 3 | You're going to learn two new keys.
Here's y on the keyboard. |

Touch the key on the Wall Chart.

| 4 | Use your right-hand pointer finger.
Watch me reach up, tap y, and return HOME. |

| 5 | Get ready. |

Instruct students in a rhythmic manner.

| 6 | Tap y ... HOME ... y ... HOME ... y ... HOME. |

| 7 | Let's practice with SPACES. |

yyy ... HOME   yyy ... HOME   yyy ... HOME   yyy ... HOME
yyy ... HOME   yyy ... HOME   jyj   jyj   jyj   jyj
jyj   jyj   jyj   jyj   jyj   jyj   jyj   jyj

Lesson 26 • y z

8 Now let's learn z.

Touch the key on the Wall Chart.

9 Use your left-hand little finger.
Watch me reach down, tap z, and return HOME.

10 Get ready.

Instruct students in a rhythmic manner.

11 Tap z ... HOME ... z ... HOME ... z ... HOME.

12 Let's practice with SPACES.

zzz ... HOME	zzz ... HOME	zzz ... HOME	zzz ... HOME
zzz ... HOME	zzz ... HOME	aza aza	aza aza
aza aza	aza aza	aza aza	aza aza

13 Let's practice with both keys.
Get ready.

14

yyy ... HOME	yyy ... HOME	yyy ... HOME	yyy ... HOME
yyy ... HOME	jyj jyj	jyj jyj	jyj jyj
jyj jyj	zzz ... HOME	zzz ... HOME	zzz ... HOME
zzz ... HOME	zzz ... HOME	aza aza	aza aza
aza aza	aza aza	zza zza	azz ... HOME
zaz ... HOME	jyh ... HOME	jyn ... HOME	juy ... HOME

Practice

1 Listen: Yes, you ran all the way to Yellowstone.
You will enter words as I spell them.
Get ready.

Say and spell each word in Step 2.
Pause and say "SPACE" when appropriate.
Say "RETURN" at the end of the line.
Adjust dictation rate to the students' skill level.

2 Yes, you ran all the way to Yellowstone.
Liz did crazy, zany zigzags with pizzazz.
Way yonder a lazy zombie yodeled loudly.

3 Open your *Flip Book* to Lesson 26.
Enter each line twice.
Tap RETURN at the end of each line.
Don't correct mistakes.
When you finish, enter the text in Bonus Lesson 26 twice.
You may begin.

Monitor the class for correct keyboarding technique:
☑ *Clear ... seat ... feet ... fingers.*
☑ *Correct reach, anchoring, and return HOME.*
☑ *Using correct fingers for each SHIFT.*

End of Lesson 26

Lesson 27

Review

Materials

Student Flip Book

Key Review

1 Check your keyboarding position.

Pause and check.

2 Clear ... seat ... feet ... fingers.

3 Let's review.
Get ready.

4
yyy ... HOME	zzz ... HOME	ppp ... HOME	xxx ... HOME
yyy ... HOME	zzz ... HOME	ppp ... HOME	xxx ... HOME
jyj aza	p;p ... HOME	sxs jyj	aza aza
p;p ... HOME	sxs sxs	jmy ... HOME	aza p?;
swx ... HOME	jhy ... HOME	p;? ... HOME	sxw ... HOME

Practice

1 Listen: Elizabeth heard jazz while eating pizza.
You will enter words as I spell them.
Get ready.

Say and spell each word in Step 2.
Pause and say "SPACE" when appropriate.
Say "RETURN" at the end of the line.
Adjust dictation rate to the students' skill level.

2 Elizabeth heard jazz while eating pizza.
Do you play in yucky, messy alleys?
The lazy, dozing lizard amazed Larry.

3 Open your *Flip Book* to Lesson 27.
Enter each line twice.
Tap RETURN at the end of each line.
Don't correct mistakes.
When you finish, enter the text in Bonus Lesson 27 twice.
You may begin.

Monitor the class for correct keyboarding technique:
☑ *Clear ... seat ... feet ... fingers.*
☑ *Correct reach, anchoring, and return HOME.*
☑ *Using correct fingers for each SHIFT.*

End of Lesson 27

Lesson 28 • q QUOTATION MARK

Lesson 28

Keys Introduced

q   QUOTATION MARK

Materials

Keyboard Wall Chart
Student Flip Book

Key Review

1 | Check your keyboarding position.

Pause and check.

2 | Clear … seat … feet … fingers.

3 | Let's review.
Get ready.

4 |
yyy … HOME	zzz … HOME	ppp … HOME	xxx … HOME
ppp … HOME	yyy … HOME	xxx … HOME	jyj jyj,
aza aza	;p; ;p;	sxs sxs	zaz … HOME
swx … HOME	sxw, jym	jym, ;p?	zaz … HOME

Keyboard Success Teacher's Guide

Key Introduction: q QUOTATION MARK

1 Check your keyboarding position.

Pause and check.

2 Clear ... seat ... feet ... fingers.

3 You're going to learn two new keys.
Here's q on the keyboard.

Touch the key on the Wall Chart.

4 Use your left-hand little finger.
Watch me reach up, tap q, and return HOME.

5 Get ready.

Instruct students in a rhythmic manner.

6 Tap q ... HOME ... q ... HOME ... q ... HOME.

7 Let's practice with SPACES.
qqq ... HOME	qqq ... HOME	qqq ... HOME	qqq ... HOME
qqq ... HOME	qqq ... HOME	aqa aqa	aqa aqa
aqa aqa	aqa aqa	aqa aqa	aqa aqa

Lesson 28 • q QUOTATION MARK

8 | Now let's learn the QUOTATION MARK.
Here's the QUOTATION MARK on the keyboard.

Touch the key on the Wall Chart.

9 | This key has two characters. Use LEFT SHIFT to enter a QUOTATION MARK.
Use your right-hand little finger and hold LEFT SHIFT down.
Watch me hold down the LEFT SHIFT, reach over, tap QUOTATION MARK, and return HOME.
Release LEFT SHIFT.

10 | Get ready.

Instruct students in a rhythmic manner.

11 | LEFT SHIFT, tap QUOTATION MARK … QUOTATION MARK … QUOTATION MARK.

12 | Let's practice with SPACES.

""" … HOME	""" … HOME	""" … HOME	""" … HOME
""" … HOME	""" … HOME	";" … HOME	";" … HOME
";" … HOME	";" … HOME	";" … HOME	";" … HOME

- *The style of quotation marks output by your students' computers or other keyboarding devices may differ from those shown here. Some settings will produce the "straight" quotation marks ("); others will produce "curly" quotation marks (" ").*

13 | Let's practice with both keys.
Get ready.

Keyboard Success Teacher's Guide

14

qqq ... HOME	qqq ... HOME	qqq ... HOME	qqq ... HOME
aqa aqa	aqa aqa	aqa aqa	aqa aqa
""" ... HOME	""" ... HOME	""" ... HOME	""" ... HOME
";" ... HOME	";" ... HOME	";" ... HOME	;"; ;";
aqz ... HOME	aqz ... HOME	;"; aqa	;"? ... HOME

Practice

1 Listen: Queen Janice quarreled about the quarter.
You will enter words as I spell them. Get ready.

Say and spell each word in Step 2.
Pause and say "SPACE" when appropriate.
Say "RETURN" at the end of the line.
Adjust dictation rate to the students' skill level.

2 Queen Janice quarreled about the quarter.
Gwen yelled, "Quit those quiz questions."
"A square of my quilt qualified to win."

3 Open your *Flip Book* to Lesson 28.
Enter each line twice.
Tap RETURN at the end of each line.
Don't correct mistakes.
When you finish, enter the text in Bonus Lesson 28 twice.
You may begin.

Monitor the class for correct keyboarding technique:
☑ *Clear ... seat ... feet ... fingers.*
☑ *Correct reach, anchoring, and return* HOME.
☑ *Using correct fingers for each* SHIFT.

End of Lesson 28

128

Lesson 29 • v APOSTROPHE

Lesson 29

Keys Introduced

V   APOSTROPHE

Materials

Keyboard Wall Chart
Student Flip Book

Key Review

| 1 | Check your keyboarding position. |

Pause and check.

| 2 | Clear ... seat ... feet ... fingers. |

| 3 | Let's review.
Get ready. |

| 4 | yyy ... HOME   qqq ... HOME   """ ... HOME   zzz ... HOME
qqq ... HOME   aqa   aqa   ;";   ;";   jyj   jyj
aza   aza   aqz ... HOME   aqz ... HOME   ;"p ... HOME
;"p ... HOME   jyh ... HOME   jyh ... HOME   jyh ... HOME |

Keyboard Success Teacher's Guide

Key Introduction: v APOSTROPHE

| 1 | Check your keyboarding position.

Pause and check.

| 2 | Clear ... seat ... feet ... fingers.

| 3 | You're going to learn two new keys. Here's v on the keyboard.

Touch the key on the Wall Chart.

| 4 | Use your left-hand pointer finger.
Watch me reach down, tap v, and return HOME.

| 5 | Get ready.

Instruct students in a rhythmic manner.

| 6 | Tap v ... HOME ... v ... HOME ... v ... HOME.

| 7 | Let's practice with SPACES.
vvv ... HOME   vvv ... HOME   vvv ... HOME   vvv ... HOME
vvv ... HOME   vvv ... HOME   fvf   fvf   fvf   fvf
fvf   fvf   fvf   fvf   fvf   fvf   fvf   fvf

| 8 | Now let's learn APOSTROPHE.

Lesson 29 • v APOSTROPHE

Touch the key on the Wall Chart.

9 | Use your right-hand little finger.
Watch me reach over, tap APOSTROPHE and return HOME.

10 | Get ready.

Instruct students in a rhythmic manner.

11 | Tap APOSTROPHE ... HOME ... APOSTROPHE ... HOME ... APOSTROPHE ... HOME.

12 | Let's practice with SPACES.
''' ... HOME   ''' ... HOME   ''' ... HOME   ''' ... HOME
''' ... HOME   ''' ... HOME   ;';   ;';   ;';   ;';
;';   ;';   ;';   ;';   ;';   ;';   ;';   ;';

- The style of apostrophe output by your students' computers or other keyboarding devices may differ from those shown here. Some settings will produce the "straight" apostrophe ('); others will produce "curly" apostrophes (' ').

13 | Let's practice with both keys. Get ready.

14 | vvv ... HOME   vvv ... HOME   vvv ... HOME   vvv ... HOME
vvv ... HOME   fvf   fvf   fvf   fvf   fvf   fvf
fvf   fvf   ''' ... HOME   ''' ... HOME   ''' ... HOME
''' ... HOME   ''' ... HOME   ''' ... HOME   ;';   ;';
;';   ;';   ;';   ;';   ;';   ;';   fvr ... HOME
fvr ... HOME   ;'p ... HOME   v's   v's   fbv ... HOME

Keyboard Success Teacher's Guide

Practice

1
Listen: Vicky's friend Steve will vote for Val.
You will enter words as I spell them.
Get ready.

Say and spell each word in Step 2.
Pause and say "SPACE" when appropriate.
Say "RETURN" at the end of the line.
Adjust dictation rate to the students' skill level.

2
Vicky's friend Steve will vote for Val.
Isn't Vic's brother driving? Let's go.
Val's van has five shelves, doesn't it?

3
Open your *Flip Book* to Lesson 29.
Enter each line twice.
Tap RETURN at the end of each line.
Don't correct mistakes.
When you finish, enter the text in Bonus Lesson 29 twice.
You may begin.

Monitor the class for correct keyboarding technique:
☑ *Clear ... seat ... feet ... fingers.*
☑ *Correct reach, anchoring, and return HOME.*
☑ *Using correct fingers for each SHIFT.*

End of Lesson 29

Lesson 30 • Review and Timed Practice

Lesson 30

Review and Timed Practice

Materials

Watch/clock with a second hand
Student Flip Book

1 | Today is your last keyboarding lesson.

Key Review

1 | Check your keyboarding position.

Pause and check.

2 | Clear ... seat ... feet ... fingers.

3 | Let's review.
Get ready.

4 |

vvv ... HOME	''' ... HOME	qqq ... HOME	""" ... HOME
qqq ... HOME	''' ... HOME	vvv ... HOME	""" ... HOME
fvf ;';	aqa ;";	aqa ;';	fvf ;";
fvr ... HOME	;'? ... HOME	azq ... HOME	;p' ... HOME
aqz ... HOME	;?" ... HOME	ftv ... HOME	;p' ... HOME

Keyboard Success Teacher's Guide

Practice

| 1 | Listen: Big planes can't zoom by the new tower.
You will enter words as I spell them.
Get ready.

Say and spell each word in Step 2.
Pause and say "SPACE" when appropriate.
Say "RETURN" at the end of the line.
Adjust dictation rate to the students' skill level.

| 2 | Big planes can't zoom by the new tower.
Didn't my ax zip through the black wood?
Won't Elizabeth, John, and Mark report?

| 3 | Open your *Flip Book* to Lesson 30.
Enter each line twice.
Tap RETURN at the end of each line.
Don't correct mistakes.
When you finish, enter each line in Bonus Lesson 30 twice.
You may begin.

Monitor the class for correct keyboarding technique:
☑ *Clear ... seat ... feet ... fingers.*
☑ *Correct reach, anchoring, and return HOME.*
☑ *Using correct fingers for each SHIFT.*

Lesson 30 • Review and Timed Practice

Keyboarding Rate

- *This lesson includes timed practice for keys introduced in Lessons 2–29. To accurately measure students' progress in the program, it is important to obtain this data.*

- *You will need a watch or a clock with a second hand.*

- *Important Note: The following script assumes that students will save their timed practice drills to a disk for you to check on screen or in printed form after the lesson. If the equipment students are using will not save files or if you prefer to collect this information in another manner, you will need to adjust the following instructions.*

| 1 | You're going to practice keyboarding as quickly and accurately as you can for 1 minute. You won't be graded; but I will compare your keyboarding speed in this exercise with your rate in the last timed exercise, so type quickly but carefully. |

| 2 | Look at Bonus Lesson 30 again. |

Check.

| 3 | Touch the group of three lines. |

Check.

4 | When I say begin, type the three lines one after the other as many times as you can.
Tap RETURN at the end of each line.
Try not to look at your fingers.
Don't correct mistakes.
I will stop you after 1 minute.

5 | Check your keyboarding position.

Pause.

6 | Ready ... begin.

Allow 1 minute.

7 | Stop.

Have students save their timed keyboarding work to a disk to hand in.

8 | Now save your work to your disk and leave the disk with me.

After the lesson, review the students' work, either on screen or in printed form, for speed and accuracy.

Lesson 30 • Review and Timed Practice

Calculating Gross Words A Minute (GWAM)

1 Count the total number of full lines typed during the 1-minute interval and place on Line A.

Multiply the number of lines by 6 to obtain a preliminary word count. (Each line contains the equivalent of 6 words or 30 characters.) Place on Line B.

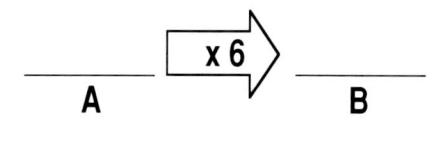

2 Count the number of letters, punctuation marks, and spaces in a partially typed line. Place on Line C.

Divide the number of characters by 5 to calculate the number of words in the partially typed line. Place on Line D.

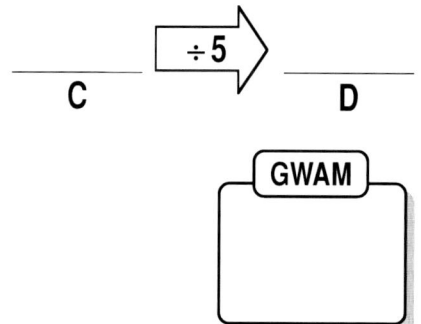

3 Add Lines B & D to obtain student's GWAM.

Record this number in the first column for Lesson 30 on the Record Grid for Handwriting and Keyboarding Rates.

In the second column of the Record Grid, record the total number of words typed without error.

You may wish to provide students with a written report for each timed practice. A template for this purpose is provided in the Appendix. Copy and complete one form for each student.

End of Lesson 30

Appendix

References

Borthwick, A.G. (1993, April). *Effects of keyboarding/typewriting on the language arts skills of elementary school students.* Paper presented at the meeting of the American Educational Research Association, Atlanta, GA. (ERIC No. ED 358 473)

Boyce, B.L., & Whitman, P.D. (1987). *Facilitator handbook for elementary keyboarding.* Pomona: Business Education Center, California State Polytechnic University.

Bartholome, L. (1984). Keyboarding—A need in today's classroom. *Printout, 2*(1), 1, 3.

Cochran-Smith, M. (1991). Word processing and writing in elementary classrooms: A critical review of related literature. *Review of Educational Research, 61*(1), 107–155.

Davidson, L.J., & Kockmann, B.J. (1995). Integrating technology into the elementary curriculum. *Business Education Forum, 50,* 26–29.

Erthal, M.J. (1985). The status of keyboarding. *Journal of Business Education, 60*(5), 192–193.

Fidanque, A., & Sullivan, G. (1985). *Word processing: Writing with computer.* Eugene School District 4J proposed computer curriculum. Eugene, OR: Eugene School District 4J.

Hansen, K. (1985). *Guidelines for the instruction of keyboarding.* Puyallup, WA: Puyallup School District.

Hedley, P. (1985, October). Once more: The keyboarding debate. *Business Exchange.*

Jackson, T.H., & Berg, D. (1986). Elementary keyboarding—Is it important? *The Computing Teacher, 13*(6), 8–11

Kisner, E. (1984). Keyboarding—A must in tomorrow's world. *The Computing Teacher, 11*(6), 21–22.

McGarvey, J. (1986). Is it time to boot out cursive writing? *Classroom Computer Learning, 6*(6), 36–37.

Prigge, L., & Braathen, S. (1993). Working with elementary students in keyboarding. *Business Education Forum, 48,* 33–35.

Robinson, J.W. (1985, Spring). Elementary keyboarding: Some factors to consider. *Century 21 Reporter,* 2–4.

Robinson, J.W., & others. (1991). *Paws presents computer keyboarding* (2nd ed.). Cincinnati, OH: South-Western Publishing Co.

Rhodes, G.S. (1986). Keyboarding—The keystone of computer literacy. *The Balance Sheet, 67,* 4.

Sormunen, C. (1984). Inservice workshops: One answer to the issue of elementary school keyboarding. *Journal of Business Education, 60*(1), 14–17.

Sormunen, C. (1993). Learning style: An analysis of factors affecting keyboarding achievement of elementary school students. *Delta Pi Epsilon Journal, 35*(1), 26–38.

Warner, K., Behymer, J., & McCrary, S. (1992). Two points of view on elementary keyboarding. *Business Education Forum, 47,* 27–33.

Wetzel, K. (1985). Keyboarding skills: Elementary my dear teacher? *The Computing Teacher, 12*(9), 15–19.

Wood, B., & Freeman, F. (1932). *An experiment study of the educational influences of the typewriter in the elementary school.* New York: Macmillan.

Handwriting Rate Worksheet

Name _____ Date _____ Number of Words _____

Did the quick, brown fox jump?
Is there time for some people?
Magician Vic can zap all yaks.

_____

_____

_____

_____

_____

_____

_____

_____

_____

_____

_____

_____

Keyboard
Success

Record Grid for Handwriting and Keyboarding Rates

Student	Lesson 1		Lesson 7		Lesson 16		Lesson 23		Lesson 30	
	Total Words	Legible Words	Total Words	Correct Words	Total Words	Correct Words	Total Words	Correct Words	Total Words	Correct Words

Keyboard Success

Position Chart for Good Keyboarding Habits

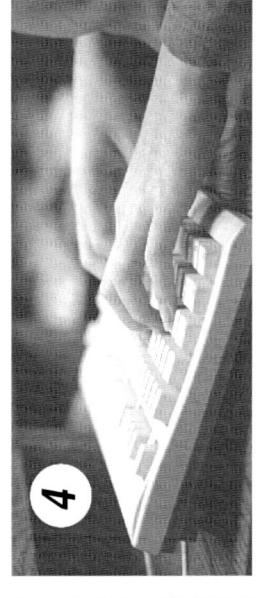

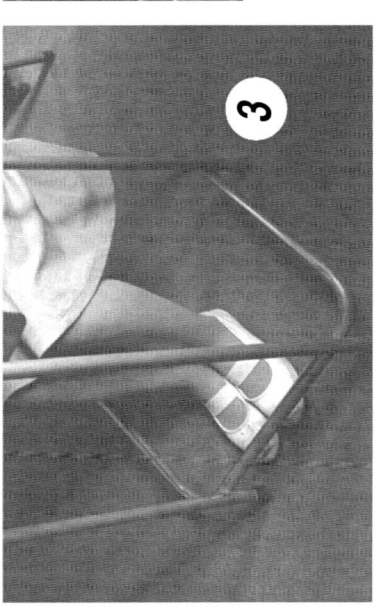

1 CLEAR
work area

2 SEAT
- sit up straight
- elbows in
- one handspan away

3 FEET
and chair flat on floor

4 FINGERS
- wrists flat
- fingers curved
- fingertips on keys

Keyboard Success

Finger Naming Worksheet

Match each finger with the correct name. Write the name on the line by that finger. Copy names from the word box.

thumb   ring   pointer   middle   little

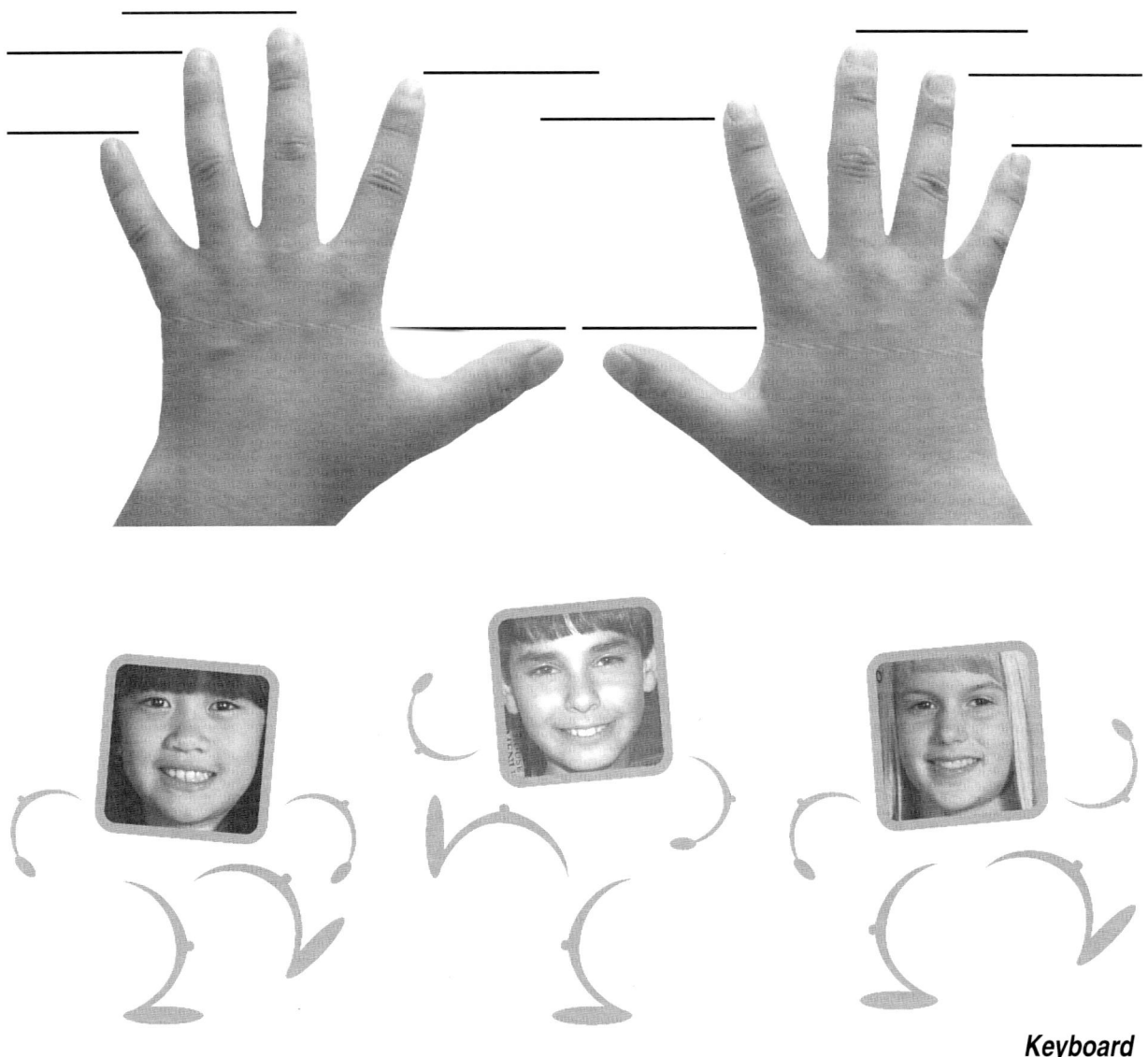

Keyboard
Success

Keyboard Template

Keyboard Success

Calculating Gross Words A Minute (GWAM)

Keyboard Success

Student _____ Date _____

1 Count the total number of full lines typed during the 1-minute interval and place on Line A.

Multiply the number of lines by 6 to obtain a preliminary word count. (Each line contains the equivalent of 6 words or 30 characters.) Place on Line B.

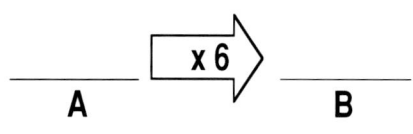

2 Count the number of letters, punctuation marks, and spaces in a partially typed line. Place on Line C.

Divide the number of characters by 5 to calculate the number of words in the partially typed line. Place on Line D.

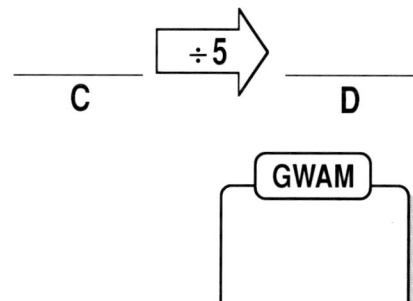

3 Add Lines B & D to obtain student's GWAM.

Calculating Gross Words A Minute (GWAM)

Keyboard Success

Student _____ Date _____

1 Count the total number of full lines typed during the 1-minute interval and place on Line A.

Multiply the number of lines by 6 to obtain a preliminary word count. (Each line contains the equivalent of 6 words or 30 characters.) Place on Line B.

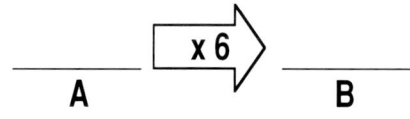

2 Count the number of letters, punctuation marks, and spaces in a partially typed line. Place on Line C.

Divide the number of characters by 5 to calculate the number of words in the partially typed line. Place on Line D.

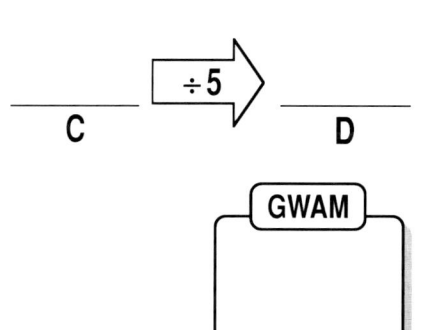

3 Add Lines B & D to obtain student's GWAM.

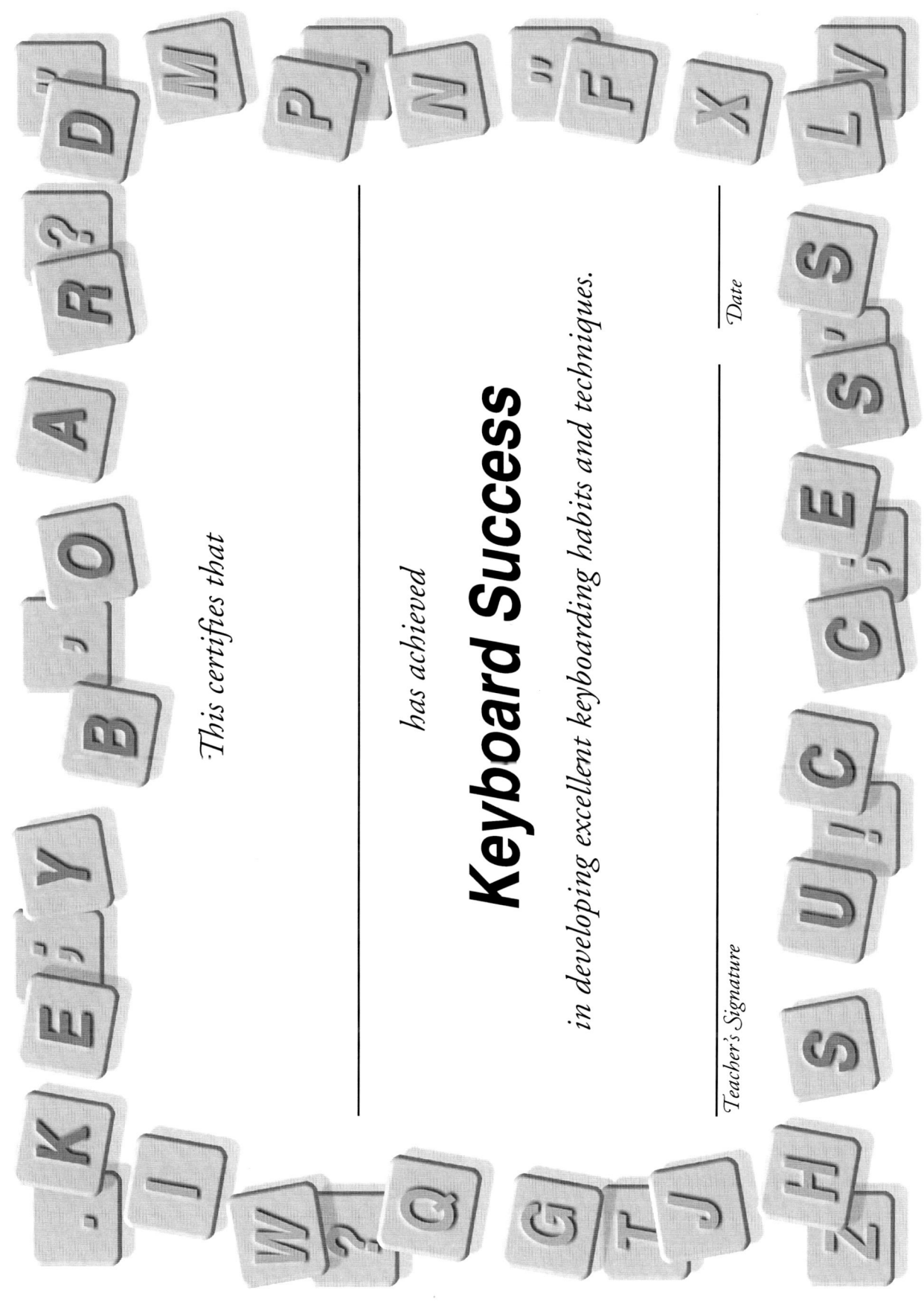